What They Know about . . .

PARENTING!

D1565061

Hay House Titles of Related Interest

What They Know about . . .

PARENTING!

Celebrity Moms and Dads
Give Us Their Take on Having Kids

Interviews by Cindy Pearlman

Edited by Jill Kramer

HAY HOUSE, INC.
Carlsbad, California
London • Sydney • Johannesburg
Vancouver • Hong Kong • New Delhi

Published and distributed in the United States by: Hay House, Inc.: www.hayhouse.com • **Published and distributed in Australia by:** Hay House Australia Pty. Ltd.: www.hayhouse.com.au • **Published and distributed in the United Kingdom by:** Hay House UK, Ltd.: www.hayhouse.co.uk • **Published and distributed in the Republic of South Africa by:** Hay House SA (Pty), Ltd.: orders@psdprom.co.za • **Distributed in Canada by:** Raincoast: www.raincoast.com • **Published in India by:** Hay House Publishers India: www.hayhouseindia.co.in

Editorial supervision: Jill Kramer • *Design:* Tricia Breidenthal

Library of Congress Cataloging-in-Publication Data

Pearlman, Cindy.
  What they know about-- parenting! : celebrity moms and dads give us their take on having kids / interviews by Cindy Pearlman ; edited by Jill Kramer. -- 1st ed.
     p. cm.
  ISBN 978-1-4019-0898-0 (tradepaper)
  1. Parenting. 2. Child rearing. 3. Celebrities--Miscellanea. I. Kramer, Jill, II. Title.
  HQ755.8.P418 2007
  649'.1--dc22   2006101619

ISBN: 978-1-4019-0898-0

10 09 08 07   4 3 2 1
1st edition, June 2007

Printed in the United States of America

*To all the celebrity moms and dads
who contributed to this book . . .
and to parents and children
of all ages everywhere!*

C O n t e n t s

Introduction

There is child support in the form of a monthly check, and then there is another kind of child support that lasts a lifetime. It's a sprinkling of wise ingredients, a few helpful suggestions, or a nudge in the right direction. Who wouldn't like a little "sit-down," magic words, or a special secret to help with the most important role of your lifetime—being a mom or dad?

Kids don't come with directions . . . at least the ones we've run into weren't sporting manuals attached to their iPod and Rollerblade sneakers. Can you imagine if your baby came with a little instruction booklet tied to the umbilical cord called How Not to Mess Me Up Before I Turn 18. No Further Assembly Required? (Hey, we want one of those in the waterproof, indestructible version.) *If only it were that easy.* Life would be pretty simple, and so would parenting.

Wake up for a moment, because that was just a pipe dream. Now it's time to return to the real world where your toddler Cade won't go to sleep, little Wilmer just whacked his younger sister Scout for the third time, and even the dog Sam (only dogs have normal names these days) has gone AWOL to avoid being blamed for eating that bag of rock salt in the garage. (By the way, this did happen to one parent who was told in the emergency room that her son wouldn't get sick but would have the purest urine in the Midwest for the next month. The five-year-old's reasoning: "Just 'cause." *Translation:* "Just because [insert silent scream from his mother here].")

When you become a parent, it's safe to say that your child isn't the only one doing the growing up. Part of the process is realizing your shortcomings as a parent, including the fact that you don't have *all* the answers. But the happy news is that most parents have *some* of them, and darn good ones . . . which is how this book was born.

Just as you tell your kid that it's good to share, the parents in this book are happy to share their approaches to raising small, medium, and large children. (The truth is, your job is never really done even when the kids are parents themselves.)

It's funny that the advice givers in this book simply aren't the kind of people you might expect to find offering up tidbits of wisdom on raising kids. These are powerful, respected, world-famous people whose public roles aren't always connected to wiping tiny noses and potty training. These individuals are known for playing other roles in public . . . as actors, actresses, directors, news anchors, media celebrities, business tycoons, top editors, journalists, authors, and activists.

These are people you might think don't have to worry about raising their own kids because they could have someone such as a high-priced nanny do it for them. Our star voices don't cop to that one. They consider parenting to be their number one reason for being on this earth—their calling, their sacred responsibility, and the reason why they wake up happy (although sometimes yawning) each morning. They have the same parental dilemmas as anyone else out there, including little Johnny catching five minutes of *Bad Santa* on HBO and now perhaps being scarred for life.

Like most (if not all) parents, nobody here possesses all of the answers, but each mom and dad seems to have perfected a way of getting through a few of the universal rough spots, and they want to pass on what they know and what works for them.

This book is about more than what to put in the diaper bag or when to send someone to bed. It also offers emotional support for those moments of overwhelming guilt or mind-boggling exhaustion. We thought that it would help if you heard someone else you might admire say, "I've also been pulling my hair out."

When asked for tips about juggling work and family life, even the beautiful Catherine Zeta-Jones sighs and says she's not Wonder Woman when it comes to working and raising her children, Dylan and Carys. "People ask me how I juggle a career with motherhood. I don't juggle well at all. It's called scheduling. You have to look forward to the chaos and plan the logistics of it all. My life is about: 'Where do I find a sandbox to entertain my son after I do a scene?'"

There are the new parents who are figuring out how to become someone's mommy or daddy without freaking out. New pop and actor Jack Black says that he has real fears about raising his infant son: "It's scary. I haven't read any books on the subject. What if I mess up?"

Actress Melissa Joan Hart echoes his feelings, admitting, "When I first got pregnant, I freaked out. I had to remind myself, *I'm turning 30.* I guess I still see myself as this little 16-year-old."

There are other new fathers who are in awe of the changes in their lives, including the pop to little Violet Affleck. "I love being a father," Ben Affleck says. "It's wonderful, and it has completely changed my life. I know you've heard this a million times and it sounds clichéd, but being a father is the most important thing in my life. It reorganized my priorities." Ben tells us a hilarious tidbit about feeding Violet later in the book.

Die Hard tough guy Bruce Willis admits that fatherhood changed his perspective and made him feel like less of a star in his own universe, even if he is an A-list actor in Hollywood. He shares his thoughts in these pages.

New dad Hugh Jackman says that he never knew a human being could be so completely dependent on him until he and his wife adopted little Oscar. Yes, it does freak him out a bit. "The thing with a baby is that he's so completely dependent on you that it creates this newfound worry," he says. "Even when you're watching TV, you imagine that things are going wrong with the baby. I don't know how I control it, but you just become like a lion wanting to protect the cub."

How do you survive all the worries that come with being a parent? Denzel Washington found some words of wisdom from Geraldo Rivera. Read about what was said later in the book, because it was very informative to this father who's raising four great kids with his wife.

Of course, we also delight in the lighter sides of raising children. Rosie O'Donnell admits, "When I'm in a group of adults at a dinner party, I actually say, 'Excuse me, I gotta go peeps.' Why am I saying that? I'm the grown-up!"

Hugh Jackman says, "I think a large part of being a father for me now is changing pooey nappies. I can't even believe I'm saying the words *pooey nappies*." Then he sobers and continues,

"I'd change pooey nappies all day long, because my kids have no concept about life or any other desire except for the fact that I'm their dad and they need me. This is the greatest thing of all time."

That's the catch with the lighter side of parenting: It only lasts a minute before the profound part seeps back in.

Kate Hudson says that being with her son is life itself, and you'll read her beautiful words about young Ryder later on.

Time-out for a second while we explain a different kind of birth. This book was born when we—that is, book editor Jill Kramer and celebrity journalist Cindy Pearlman—talked over the phone about a parenting book. We realized that it doesn't really matter if someone is a celebrity, a "civilian," or a single mother or father . . . parenting is a topic that brings up common feelings in just about all moms and dads: love, trepidation, angst, tenderness, frustration, wonderment, sadness, delight, and much more.

This book was born to jump Keds-first into the humorous, often heartbreaking, always thoughtful, and occasionally embarrassing moments of being a parent. The idea was that the accounts presented here would be truly entertaining, relatable, and helpful.

Try the suggestions you think might make sense and dismiss those that don't fit into your family. And we invite you to sympathize with the plight of your fellow parents. One of our favorite "Daddy dilemmas" comes from original cool guy

David Letterman, who admits that he was more than a little bit nervous driving baby Harry home from the hospital. We're sure it's gotten easier since that day (uh . . . at least we think so, Dave).

The book has longer stories and bits of advice, as well as quick words of wisdom and concise quotes that we call *Time-Outs.*

This work is for all parents—no matter if your kids are toddlers, teens, or baby boomers. So open up the book anywhere . . . and prepare to laugh, cry, nod your head in agreement, and ache with empathy and joy.

In the end, there is no perfect way to parent. *If only.* There's just trial and error; and when it's mixed with a lot of love, you really can't go wrong.

If you're reading this while your child is howling and demanding to know why he or she must stop trying to ride on the back of the family cat, we can offer another way of telling your little one why he or she must listen to you. . . .

In the immortal words of a rock-salt-eating five-year-old, "Just 'cause."

They give the baby to you and let you drive it home.
You look in the rearview mirror and see a three-day-old
human being. This is the biggest traffic hazard ever. . . .
Later, I learned that the only thing that grounds me is the
grandmother. She knows the answer to every question.

— David Letterman

I taught them to rock climb and ride motorcycles.
They love it and they're really good athletes. They
also have to deal with the paparazzi. My kids are cool
about it—they know how to chill. It's strange when the
paparazzi tell me, "Yeah, Connor batted great today."

— Tom Cruise

Dr. Keith Ablow

Daddy Dossier

Dr. Keith Ablow brings both his professional and personal experience as a psychiatrist, author, husband, and father to daytime television on his daily syndicated program, *The Dr. Keith Ablow Show,* offering viewers practical solutions to everyday challenges. He has also served as an expert witness in some of the most highly publicized trials in the U.S. and has shared his expertise on numerous national TV shows, including *The Oprah Winfrey Show, Today, Good Morning America, The Tyra Banks Show,* CNN's *Larry King Live,* and Fox News Channel's *On the Record with Greta Van Susteren.*

Keith graduated from Brown University and Johns Hopkins School of Medicine. While still a medical student, he wrote his first book, *Medical School: Getting In, Staying In, Staying Human.* After receiving his M.D., Keith continued to write, publishing numerous nonfiction books, including *How to Cope with Depression, To Wrestle with Demons,* and *Anatomy of a Psychiatric Illness,* as well as magazine and newspaper articles.

Then, in 1990, after a close friend was murdered, Keith was inspired to write the first of his best-selling crime-based series of novels, *Without Mercy.* Keith's later novels include *Denial, Projection, Compulsion, Psychopath, Murder Suicide,* and *The Architect.* His most recent book, *Inside the Mind of Scott Peterson,* was a *New York Times* bestseller; and in the spring of 2007, Keith published his first self-help work, *Pain to Power: The Journey to Truth, Love and the Rest of Your Life.* He is married and has an eight-year-old daughter and a four-year-old son.

What I Know about . . . the Psyche of a Child

The first thing any parent needs to understand is that being a child is in itself frightening in the sense that you don't have a lot of effective power in the world. This means that everything you do as a parent—your loving nature or lack of love—is magnified 1,000 times by your child.

Stop for a second: Really look at your actions through the lens of your child. That's the best advice I can give anyone because it will help you make decisions about how you'll behave toward your child.

What I Know about . . .
Talking to Children

Often we want so desperately to teach our children that we tend to sit them down and tell them what we know about the world. We talk *at* them day and night. A better approach is to ask your children what they've experienced in their day and how they feel about their world. This approach teaches them that you care about their feelings—it's telling your kids that their thoughts are valuable. This also has a long-range effect, in that it teaches children to communicate with someone who truly listens to them.

When they're older, they won't settle for any less in other relationships. Remember that a parent-child relationship is the best insulation and immunity against abusive relationships in the future for your kids. They'll compare everything and everyone to whether they were well loved at home when they were young.

What I Know about . . .
Single Acts of Kindness Toward a Child

Through my private practice and on my show, I've had the benefit of speaking with thousands of adults who, of course, were once children. A very large number of them remember single acts of kindness from their child-hood. They will say to me, "Dr. Keith, even though I was five, I'll never forget the time when my mother or father did something kind for me. Let me tell you about it." As a parent, I suggest going through the day thinking, *Hmm, perhaps there's an opportunity on this day or in this hour to provide a lifelong memory through an act of kindness for my child so that he or she will someday say, "I remember the time when . . ."*

If you look, you'll find the opportunity. For example, the other day I stopped and picked two wildflowers. Handing them to my daughter, I said, "I'm the luckiest dad in the world. I never thought I'd have a little girl like you. I'm so happy." I know my children won't remember every single day of their childhood. But they *will* remember the feeling they had from our time together. Were they respected? Did I ask another question about what they just said? Did I say "I love you"? You're really telling your child through these kind acts that you're listening. It's saying to them, "It's about you. I love you. You mean the world to me, and I want to honor your feelings and thoughts."

What I Know about . . .
Losing My Temper with a Child

I understand the pressures of the day and the chaotic nature of life. There are times when my own patience is in short supply, and then I must deal with parenting issues. If you find yourself losing your temper, cop to it with your child. You should say, "I shouldn't have yelled. It was wrong and I'm sorry."

It really is okay to apologize to your kids. They can and should know that big people make mistakes, too. The other day, my daughter was being difficult with her younger brother. I was angry and said, "If you want to be a part of this family, you have to be nice to your little brother." My daughter looked at me and said, "It's not up to you to make me a part of this family. I *am* a part of this family."

She was right to correct me, because I'd given her a toxic message. It was almost as if I were saying, "Behave or we'll throw you out. You're done if you're mean to your brother." Of course that's not true, but a little mind hears it that way. That's why I had to tell her I was sorry. I told her that I still wanted her to be nice to her little brother, but I shouldn't have said that dumb thing to her.

The point is, you should lead by example. When you're wrong, say you're wrong. Your kids will learn this skill and bring that equation to their own lives. When they hurt someone on the playground or later in life through their words, they'll stop and say, "I'm sorry." They'll also know that no one is perfect. Now that's a powerful example to pass on to your children. It's like saying, "All of us have anxieties and fears, and sometimes they get the better of us. But I can stop and say I'm sorry when I've hurt someone I love."

What I Know about . . . Time Crunches

One of the toughest things about being a parent these days is the time crunch between work and family. I hear this all the time from my clients who wish they had more time for their children. I've always been very careful not to let my work eclipse my kids' soccer games or school plays. I've also been lucky enough to involve my children a bit in my work so they can see where Dad goes all day long.

When I first started my daytime talk show, my son visited me on the set. The Warner Bros. team that promoted the last *Superman* movie was still in the offices. So my son, who is four, saw a life-sized stand-up of Superman right next to a life-sized stand-up of Dad. My son got wide-eyed and said, "Dad, I didn't know, but during the day, you're a superhero!"

Part of me wanted to say, "Yes, that's true, son. I get in the car in the morning, leave the house, and do my superhero duties." But I figured that wasn't the best way . . . so I was honest with him.

Time-out

My best parenting advice is that I've always told my children to "use the difficult." This means that anything that goes wrong in life can be turned to your advantage, no matter how disastrous it is. I told my girls this for the first time when they were little, and I've repeated it often over the years to the point where my kids eventually made a pillow cushion with USE THE DIFFICULT embroidered on it.

"Use the difficult" is great advice for both your children and for you, the parent. It's good life advice because basically you're telling your child that you must see the positive in what went wrong. The deal is: The negativity is already there . . . you're living with it. If you just look for the positive, you'll begin again. And isn't that what life is really made up of—starting again and again from a position of positivity and feeling like you can do anything? What better lesson can a parent teach a child?

— Michael Caine

When I was a kid, my parents moved a lot, but I always found them.

— Rodney Dangerfield

Ben Affleck

Daddy Dossier

Boston native Ben Affleck grew up in Cambridge, Massachusetts, where his father worked as a social worker and his mother was a schoolteacher. Ben entered show business as a child by starring in a Burger King commercial and then in a PBS miniseries. He broke into movies with roles in *Dazed and Confused*, *Mallrats,* and *Chasing Amy.*

In 1996, Ben decided to bunk on the couch of his good friend Matt Damon. Together, they wrote the script for *Good Will Hunting,* which resulted in a hit movie and earned them an Academy Award® for Best Original Screenplay. (They took their moms as dates to the Oscars.) Ben went on to star in blockbusters including *Armageddon, Pearl Harbor,* and *The Sum of All Fears.* He's married to actress Jennifer Garner, and they are the proud parents of baby Violet Anne, who is destined to grow up to be a Boston Red Sox fan.

What I Know about . . .
Feeding My Daughter

I'll never forget when my wife, Jennifer, had to work on a film and I was at home taking care of the baby for the first time by myself. Jennifer ran out of the bedroom and said, "Honey, you know how to feed her solid food, don't you? You take the peaches and mix it with the oatmeal. You mix it up, okay? The peaches and the oatmeal. And then you get a bowl out. You put both the peaches and the oatmeal in the bowl, take a spoon, and mix."

She looked at me in all seriousness and then asked, "Is this too complicated for you?"

Actually, making the mush *wasn't* too complicated. But the thought that my wife thinks it might be too hard for me to mix peaches and oatmeal speaks to something—what, I'm not sure.

*Come on, it's just mashing a banana. What
is Ben doing? Giving her a mouthful of spaghetti?
Giving her an entire forkful? I'm going to talk to him.*

— **Matt Damon,** joking about his buddy Ben's
"What I Know . . ." story

Antonio Banderas

Daddy Dossier

So what if he's an award-winning actor? The only thing his kids care about is that Antonio Banderas voices Puss in Boots in the megapopular *Shrek* series. The handsome actor grew up in Málaga, Spain, and got his break doing theater in Madrid before being cast in Spanish films. American audiences were introduced to him when he starred in *The Mambo Kings,* played Armand in *Interview with the Vampire,* and was Tom Hanks's significant other in the critically acclaimed *Philadelphia.*

Antonio met his wife, actress Melanie Griffith, on the set of their film *Two Much* in 1995. He played Che in the big-screen adaptation of *Evita* and also had roles in *Spy Kids, Frida, Once Upon a Time in Mexico, And Starring Pancho Villa as Himself, Imagining Argentina, The Mask of Zorro, The Legend of Zorro, Take the Lead,* and *Bordertown.* He is stepfather to Melanie's children, Alexander Bauer and Dakota Johnson; and is "Poppi" to his daughter with Melanie, Stella, 10.

What I Know about . . .
Learning from My Child

I learn more from my daughter Stella than she learns from me. I live to serve her and my older kids, too. I can easily go back to those young years in my mind. I can see what she's going through, and I just want to be there to help. She's getting so much older, and she doesn't need Poppi so much every minute. That breaks my heart. The time really does go by so fast. You shouldn't miss a minute of it.

What I Know about . . .
Being Large and in Charge

The truth is, I'm not strict—no way. My wife, Melanie, is actually the stricter one. The reason for that is because two of my children are stepchildren. Dakota is Melanie's daughter with Don [Johnson]. She's 16. Alexander [Melanie's son with actor Steven Bauer] is 21. Alexander and I communicate about women. But I always tell them, "You have a father. He's important to you."

With Stella, my own blood, I don't believe in being strict. Talking to her is a really good thing. I talk to her like she's an adult. That way, she doesn't hide things like "What can I give Poppi and what don't I give Poppi?" Everything is open.

When I talk to my little Stella about something serious, I talk to her like she's an adult; I talk to her like a man talking to another person. She totally picks up on the idea that you don't need to point and scream. If you're too strict, the kids hide things, as in "This is what I can give Poppi, and this is what I keep from him." I want it all out on the table. I don't ground them, either. You can achieve much better results from just sitting down calmly and discussing the issue. It's really about resolving the problem—that's the key."

I adopted and I had an epidural.

— **Rosie O'Donnell**

*The first time, I was going
to get the epidural in the seventh month.*

— **Joely Richardson**

Benjamin Bratt

Daddy Dossier

Benjamin Bratt, who is part Peruvian and part German, is the middle child of five and grew up in San Francisco. His mother is a Native American activist and nurse. His father was a "tin knocker," or a sheet-metal worker. Benjamin studied the arts at the University of California, Santa Barbara, and at the American Conservatory Theater in San Francisco. He got his early break on TV with the series *Knightwatch,* which aired in the late '80s. He is best known for playing Detective Rey Curtis on the hit NBC series *Law & Order.*

Benjamin received raves for playing Miguel Piñero in *Piñero.* He also starred in *One Good Cop, Bound by Honor, Traffic, Miss Congeniality, The Next Best Thing, Red Planet, Catwoman,* and *The Woodsman.* He is married to model and actress Talisa Soto. Their daughter, Sophia Rosalinda Bratt, was born in 2002; and their son, Mateo Bravery, was born in 2005.

What I Know about . . .
Daddy Basics

Just be loving. You also have to recognize that you need to take the focus off yourself and put it on your children to give them a proper start in life.

Listen, it sounds corny to say, but why are we in a society that's so rife with disorder and emotional disease? Why do we have so many people who wound other people? It's because somewhere along the way we, as a society, forgot how to parent well. We forgot how to treat one another. Unfortunately, that which is learned is passed on to the next generation. I was very fortunate to have a set of parents who made it clear that family is what you are.

What I Know about . . . Priorities

I want to be a good husband and an amazing father. I can't do that if I'm off in South America for four months holding only a telephone. Now every single night I get to come home and hold my wife and daughter. You have to be there, and you can't do it long-distance.

What I Know about . . . Parental Growth

Getting married and having a child with Talisa has changed my life entirely. I've learned to love more deeply. I already thought I had a pretty good notion of what love is and how to be a loving person. I grew up in an incredibly tight-knit family. Yet, being a father to a daughter and a husband to Talisa awakened things in me that I never really knew existed. It's really a magical relationship between a man and his baby. She's just two and a half, but she came out full-blown, with her own personality and her own way of looking at the world. I'm just in love with her.

What I Know about . . . Being the Meanie

I'm already a total pushover! It's going to be hard to discipline my daughter, but I'll leave that to Mom.

*I change Sam's poopy diapers. It's not a big
deal now. Once he starts eating solids, then it will
be a real bummer. But I don't mind wiping my son's
behind because it's like he's a little me and now I have
two behinds, if you know what I mean. Women should
explain the diaper change that way to their men.
It makes the whole thing much easier to grasp.*

— **Jack Black** on doing his duty with his baby son

Michael Chiklis

Daddy Dossier

Michael Chiklis grew up in Massachusetts and was educated at Brown University College of Fine Arts, where he majored in acting. After graduation, he hightailed it to New York City, where he was cast in theater roles. His film break was being cast as the late John Belushi in the movie *Wired.* Michael went on to star in two TV series, *Daddio* and *The Commish.*

He lost an incredible amount of weight at his wife's suggestion, shaved his head, and then auditioned to play tough detective Vic Mackey for the FX series *The Shield.* He won the role on what later became a hit show. Michael has also played Curly in the TV-movie version of *The Three Stooges;* and he was Ben Grimm, aka The Thing, in the hit franchise movie *Fantastic Four.*

Along with his beloved wife, Michelle, he is a parent to Autumn, 13; and Odessa, 7. Autumn plays his daughter Cassidy on *The Shield,* although her father won't allow her on set during any violent scenes. Michael also does charity work for autism groups because his character's son on *The Shield* suffers from the disease.

What I Know about . . .
Teaching Kids Honesty

My terror as a father is that I won't get it right. I don't want my kids on a therapist's couch at age 30 saying, "My dad was never there for me. He didn't have any time for me." Being a father informs what I do every single day. I want to get it right. One of the things I've tried is to have very few rules in my house. The only rule I ask my daughters to obey is simple. I've told them, "If you tell me the truth, then you'll never get into any trouble." It's simple . . . that's it.

My kids are young now—13 and 7. I started this honesty rule when they were very little girls because I wanted it to sink in before they became teenagers. You hear so many scary stories about teens stealing cars, drinking beers, or smoking joints at parties. I don't want any of that in my life. But I've told my daughters from a young age that whatever it is, if they tell me about it and are honest, then we can fix anything together and they won't get in trouble.

My biggest fear as a dad—and what would kill me— is my children not coming to me when they truly have a problem. The honesty rule means that there's always an open dialogue in our house. It also means that my girls know that what they get from home is love and support, period. I'm a softy. My kids can always come to me, and I'll help them fix it.

We live in a tough world. I know so many parents who are afraid that they're not preparing their kids for the real world. They might think that as soon as their children walk out the door and into the educational system, it's all about the school of life and hard knocks. It's true that others will make your children feel crappy and bad. I don't want any of that negativity in my home. I want them to feel like home is a cocoon. They can say anything that's in their hearts or on their minds and not worry about editing themselves. I want them to know that when they go out into the world, they have a sanctuary called home. I think that will make them stronger people.

I don't want my kids to be hard, soulless people. I want them to be soulful, and caring of others. I want them to realize that you don't have to let your problems eat away at you and harden your heart. Just tell me the truth and everything will be okay.

I'll never forget when my little Odessa was only five. Her big black pen slipped off the paper and she made a huge, ugly mark across my desk. She came around the corner in our house looking very sad and said, "Daddy, if I tell you the truth, then I won't get into trouble, right?" I told her that was absolutely true. So with her little hand in mine, she took me to see my desk and showed me what happened. I said, "Okay, honey. I'm so glad you told me the truth. You just made a mistake. We'll clean it together."

My theory is that when she becomes a teenager, she'll remember those types of moments from her childhood.

This might not work for every family, but it works for *my* family. You know, they don't give you a pamphlet with kids. It's just me trusting my instincts as a father. If I'm honest and open and available to my kids, I figure that they'll come out on top. Of course life is full of consequences—I'm not sheltering them. I'm just telling them that when they screw up and lie, then that's the worst-case scenario. I'm also telling them that when they screw up, they shouldn't fear coming home.

You should never fear coming home. That's where you'll find the people who will help you.

Time-out

*My son is going through a Daddy thing. It's
always "Dada, Dada, Dada." I'm like, "What about
me—Mama!?" I'm already doing guilt and telling him,
"I carried you around for nine months. I gave you these
boobs; they sagged for you. What did Tim do? He just
had sex with me. It was all fun for Tim. All gain."*

— **Helena Bonham Carter,**
who has a son, Billy Ray, 3, with
Charlie and the Chocolate Factory director Tim Burton

Denis Leary

Daddy Dossier

Denis Leary grew up in the Big Apple and got his start as a successful standup comic. He currently plays Tommy Gavin on the acclaimed FX series *Rescue Me*. Leary also voices Diego, the saber-toothed tiger in the hit *Ice Age* animated film series. He has starred in the movies *Wag the Dog, The Ref,* and *The Thomas Crown Affair,* among others.

Denis established the Leary Firefighters Foundation after 9/11 to help raise money for families in need. He even drove a fire truck on that fateful day when the New York City Fire Department was short on help. He is married and is the father to two sons, John Joseph, 15; and Devin, 13.

What I Know about . . .
"Go to Your Room!"

The whole "Go to your room" thing really needs to be reconsidered. That's the best place you could send your kid these days. It's not a punishment. "Go to your room" is a reward. They've got the Internet, guitars, Game Boy, and their cell phones. Now I say, "Go to the kitchen for the next three hours! *I'm* going to your room."

What I Know about . . . Summer Break

I will never make my kids do anything like go to summer camp. *Please.* When I was a kid, I grew up on the streets of New York in a real neighborhood. It was all Irish, Italian, and Puerto Rican kids. Our summers were spent in the streets with our parents screaming for us to come in for lunch and dinner.

One summer all the parents felt bad and sent all of the kids to camp up in New Hampshire. We got on this big yellow bus and drove toward something odd called trees. On the bus ride, a bunch of neighborhood kids got into this big fistfight with the suburban kids. So they sent us tougher kids back to New York City. *The same day!* We were gone approximately eight hours.

When we got back to New York, we said, "Thank God!" I mean, they had deer and other scary animals up there in New Hampshire. We were much safer on the streets of New York because we knew how to deal with *those* animals.

Okay, I did send my own kid to camp many years later. He hated it. I guess certain things are genetic.

The moral of the story is: *Don't make your kids do stuff you hated.*

Time-out

*We have a thing called "the Honesty Club."
We sit around with the kids and say, "Okay, the
Honesty Club is in session. What is said in the club
stays in the club." I'd love to tell you what has happened
in the club, but it's confidential. Those are the rules. But
the premise is honesty and that the kids can tell me
anything and not get in trouble. More than anything,
I want them to tell me everything so I can help them.*

— Garth Brooks

Kelly Preston

Mommy Material

Actress, activist, and mother Kelly Preston was born in Honolulu, Hawaii, and studied drama at the University of Southern California. She has made her mark in movies such as *Jerry Maguire, Addicted to Love, For Love of the Game,* and *Jack Frost.* Her most recent film was the country-music love story *Broken Bridges.*

Kelly is married to superstar John Travolta and is the proud mother of Jett, 15; and Ella Bleu, 7. When Jett was a little boy, he suffered from severe allergies and asthma attacks. Kelly works with the Children's Health Environmental Coalition (CHEC), a nonprofit organization whose mission is to help parents learn about environmental toxins that can affect their children's health.

What I Know about . . . Little Babies

The first thing I would tell any new mother or father is that you must get sleep when the baby sleeps. That's the only way to recharge and not walk around like a zombie. I can't stress enough that this is a huge one. I know so many moms who think that the time when the baby is sleeping should be filled with laundry and cooking. Please don't do it. Your sleep and recharging is the most important thing for your little one.

It's also really crucial to decide if you're going to use a pacifier or not. They have some that are like a nipple, and those are great ones. I used them with my own kids when they were babies.

What I Know about . . . Health and Safety

I can't stress enough that you should have as few chemicals around your babies and children as possible. Really be careful when it comes to cleaning products that you use around the house and the nursery. Think about your rug-cleaning substances because your baby will be crawling around on those carpets. This can actually be such a dangerous thing because your child has such a little body and a small immune system. What doesn't bother us as adults in big bodies isn't the same as what can affect a young child's health. So you really need to be careful to limit the chemicals that come into your home.

I found that there were great natural diapers and wipes that used few to no chemicals. These might cost a little bit more, but it's worth it to keep chemicals away from your children's systems, especially when they're growing and developing.

What I Know about . . . Temper Tantrums

I believe that you must let kids have a temper tantrum now and then. It's a way for your children to get those emotions out of their system. I do have a little trick when it comes to sugar and temper tantrums, which have been linked. I do allow sugar in my house, but I keep it to a minimum. The key is, I only allow sugar after a protein. It really does keep the tantrums down. We also allow a small amount of chocolate if our kids are already well fed. It doesn't cause temper tantrums that way.

What I Know about . . . Barney!

We love Barney in our house. It's important to me that you don't diss Barney. I've got Barney's back—you mess with me when you mess with Barney. When you see the joy on your kids' faces, then you have to love Barney. We love the Wiggles, too.

What I Know about . . . Fun

We're a dancing family. We're a goofy family. We sing the songs. Even Ella knows the words to all the *Hairspray* songs. Johnny sings them around the house. Now Ella sings them, too. There's nothing better than singing and dancing with your kids—it's like spreading joy around your entire home.

We ride bikes, go swimming, do art projects, and do other fun things as a family. We also go to Denny's. My big places to shop are Wal-Mart and Target. Seriously—that's where half of my kids' stuff comes from now. I don't get to go to the superfancy stores.

*We have a swear box in our house. If the boys
say a naughty word, then they have to pay from
their allowance. But I can be guilty, too. I saw
someone not being nice to their dog the other day.
I said something that we can't print. My kids took
me right to the swear box and told me to pay up!*

— **Pamela Anderson** on how
she keeps it "clean" at home

Laura Innes

Mommy Material

Laura Innes hails from Pontiac, Michigan, and graduated from Northwestern University, where she majored in theater. She acted in Chicago and New York for years before moving to Los Angeles, where she was discovered and cast as handicapped doctor Kerry Weaver on the hit NBC series *ER.* An accomplished director, she is also the first female contestant to win the celebrity version of *Jeopardy!*

She's married to David Brisbin and is the mother of two children, Cal, 16; and Mia, 5. Cal was three months premature and weighed only three pounds and four ounces. "He is a true miracle in my life," she says.

What I Know about . . . Opening My Ears

I guess for me the biggest thing I've learned in parenting is listening. You must take a minute to really acknowledge what your children are saying. Let's say they're screaming, "I want ice cream! I want ice cream!"

Don't react, but don't ignore them. Their wishes are important, too. I suggest that you wait a beat. *Breathe. Relax.* Listen to what they're actually saying.

The next step is not to bark out: "No, you can't have that ice cream because we're about to eat dinner!" I will say, "Honey, this isn't going to work out now. Let's move on to the next thing."

This is called *active listening.* It's really helpful to start this while your children are younger because it's a very important parenting technique in the teenage years. It's critical to really listen to what they're saying in the later years, when kids will truly test you, make you feel bad about yourself, and naturally try to break away from you. This can be very hurtful. The key is to be extra-understanding, because the children aren't trying to hurt you. You can say to your teenagers, "Oh, I know that you really wish I'd let you go to that rock concert, but unfortunately, that's not possible. Let's move on to the next thing."

Your children won't be happy because they're not getting their way. But they will be happy on one level if they feel heard and not ignored. Put yourself in their shoes for a minute. You wouldn't want to feel ignored. You wouldn't want to hear someone say, "You're driving me crazy with all that talk about the concert." You wouldn't want to hear, "How dare you ask me about that concert again!" You should acknowledge the part of them that likes to listen to music and have fun—even if their request to stay out until midnight at a rock concert will be ultimately denied by you because you're the parent and you have the last word.

What I Know about . . . Adopting

We recently adopted a child from China. Our family was ready for every problem and issue. But then we got matched up and went to get our baby. It was a time to just leap into the void, and I've never been happier than when I held my baby Mia for the first time.

What I can tell you is that overall, the babies from China do really well. Of course, as an adoptive parent, you must realize that there might be health or emotional issues. There might be other stuff, too, and you must be prepared for anything. I'm happy to report that my Mia has been such a joy. She's a healthy, funny baby and a real spitfire.

Suddenly, though, I found myself taking care of a seven-month-old while working on *ER.* I was really tired and had to figure out how to take naps, work, and care for my other child. I did have to say to my husband on occasion, "I'm sorry, honey, but I guess we're not going to that restaurant tonight." But it's worth it because the baby is such a complete joy.

As for the adoption, we did the paperwork and then waited for all the bureaucratic issues to be resolved. The waiting is very hard . . . then all of a sudden, there's a day when a door opens and they put a baby in your arms. It's exactly what everyone says in that instant. The moment you see your baby, you're overjoyed and the connection begins.

My son, my husband, and I went to China with 35 other families who were adopting. The whole thing was incredible, and we've remained close with those 35 other families and 36 babies—there was even one set of twins! You should have seen the looks on the faces of 36 babies being held by their new families. It went amazingly well, and we've all stayed in touch because it's really great for the parents and the kids to know each other. As these children get older, it answers the question, "Hey, what's happened to me in my life, and where do I come from?"

It's about very open communication when you adopt a child. I think the whole issue of "Where do I come from?" can be confusing for the child. As my daughter grows up, I want her around people who've had the same experience. The kids can interact and share feelings while they talk about their homeland. You can witness the relief on the kids' faces—even at this early age—to see children who are "just like me." We see some of the families frequently and all of them three times a year. We have a full group meeting each year to celebrate the Chinese New Year.

What I Know about . . . Sibling Rivalry

My older son, who's 16, was such a doll and so excited about his new sister, who's 5. He's incredibly sweet with her, although they do fight. I hear, "Mom, she's really bugging me. She's really irritating." He'll tell his sister, "You're so weird." But what can you do? They're siblings—with an 11-year age range between them. I allow them to work it out and don't get in the middle of it every single second. I think parents should back off a little bit when brothers and sisters fight. Kids will work it out for themselves, and they're learning an important lesson about resolving conflicts.

My son walked into the bathroom and said, "Mama, wow!" I almost broke down in tears and ruined three hours of makeup.

— **Debra Messing** on how her son, Roman, is better than fashion critic Mr. Blackwell when it comes to true compliments about style

John Tesh

Daddy Dossier

Platinum recording artist John Tesh grew up in Raleigh, North Carolina; and Long Island, New York. He began his career as a sports reporter for the *CBS Sports Spectacular* and then cohosted *Entertainment Tonight* with Mary Hart. A world-renowned singer and composer, he also hosts a syndicated radio show, *Intelligence for Your Life,* which boasts eight million listeners a week.

John is married to actress Connie Sellecca and is a stepfather to Gib, 24; and dad to their daughter, Prima, 12.

What I Know about . . .
Contracts with Your Kids

Here it is: You have to draw up a contract with your children. I have a 24-year-old named Gib and a 12-year-old named Prima. They've both signed contracts with my wife, Connie, and me over the years. We have the contracts because parents keep moving the line around, and kids really do want a handbook.

The first thing to understand is that kids are going to break the rules. It's going to happen. This is why we drew up contracts. For example, the contracts cover what happens if you come home late, what grades you're expected to get, how you're supposed to behave, the way you should talk to your parents, cursing, and so on. You go through every single thing possible.

The key is, the kids come up with the punishments. As parents, you give them a menu of possible consequences. They choose which one will fit which behavior. It's funny because every single time we suggested a punishment for a certain thing, the kids made it harder. I learned through this that kids like having a goal and want to be tough on themselves for not attaining it. When you let them choose the punishment, then it truly becomes *their* goal.

We made the kids sign the contracts and date them. I have great children, and most of the time nothing would happen for a year. Then when something did, we'd pull the actual document or contract out of the drawer.

I like this idea because let's say that your child gets a D in school. What does it mean to him or her if you bark, "You're not going to watch TV for two weeks because of your bad grades!" What does TV have to do with anything? It makes punishment very random. But if you get the children involved in the process, then they know the consequences because they chose them in the first place.

We don't pull out the contracts often, and not for the little things. Let's say you've talked back in our house or used a tone of voice—you'll get the contract pulled out. But you can appeal it before the punishment is legislated. You can also have a family meeting. In the contract, it states that anyone can call a family meeting and all four of us will sit down. Also, anyone can call a family meeting at any time. You're allowed two emergency family meetings a year. It keeps us close, and everyone in our family is involved in each other's lives.

What I Know about . . . Teenage Drivers

It's always tricky when your kids start to drive. I've read a bunch of studies that state that when your teenager has a financial stake in the automobile, then they're 40 percent less prone to have an accident. You really should have your teens pay a part of the monthly insurance or maybe 5 percent of the cost of the car. It's better for them to have a stake in the automobile rather than just borrowing Mom and Dad's car without a second thought.

Time-Out

It's hard to go on vacations with kids. I love to see them with their iPods on and carrying their computers. It's like traveling with a little deaf family, because no one talks to each other even though we're finally all in the same room. I don't like the idea of my kids texting each other while they're in the same house, either. They'll say, "Dad, please don't talk to me. I'm texting." I answer, "I know. I see you. But the person you're texting is in the next room. Did you ever think of just walking two steps and talking to your sister?"

Now, one of my rules when we take a family vacation is that you can't bring the technological stuff. It's amazing because you might think that your children would be clinging to you, crying, "Aw, Dad. I need my high-speed DSL! I need my iPod! You're ruining my life!" Within a day, though, the kids will actually be reading, playing games, and going outside to have fun with their siblings. Imagine.

— **Robin Williams**

Donald Trump

Daddy Dossier

New York native Donald Trump—aka "The Donald" —is one of the richest real-estate moguls in America. The property tycoon is the third generation to enter the family business. (Donald grew up helping his father, Fred Trump, build affordable housing.) The business genius studied finance at the University of Pennsylvania's Wharton School and decided to map out a career that was bigger than anything done before in New York City real estate. However, his billion-dollar empire hit the skids in 1990, and he declared business bankruptcy. He then did the impossible and rebuilt his empire on an even bigger scale than before.

There are many buildings around America that carry his name, and he also owns several casinos. In addition, he's the author of the best-selling books *Trump: The Art of the Comeback, Trump: The Art of the Deal,* and *Trump: How to Get Rich,* among others. A media personality with a great sense of humor, he has appeared as himself on *Roseanne, Suddenly Susan, Spin City, The Nanny, The Fresh Prince of Bel-Air,* and *The Job;* as well as in films such as

Home Alone 2: Lost in New York, Celebrity, and *54.* He also hosts the hit NBC series *The Apprentice.*

Donald is married to Slovenian model Melania Knauss and is the father of five children, Donald, Jr., 29; Ivanka, 25; Eric, 22; Tiffany, 13; and baby Barron, 1.

What I Know about . . .
Not Creating Mini-Me's

The best advice I can give to new parents is to realize immediately that your children will be unique individuals. Give them the space to be themselves and to develop their own personalities and characteristics. Just because you have a certain mind-set doesn't mean they will, too. However, realize that kids learn by example. I'm a disciplined person, and so are my children. I learned that from the example set by my own parents, and it's a good trait to pass along.

What I Know about . . .
Not Sheltering My Kids

I want them to go through the whole gamut. They'll have good times and bad. I hope they'll handle the bad times—a lot of my friends couldn't. I want my children to have as many good times as possible, but in a lifetime, you'll always have bad times. You have to learn how to cope with both.

What I Know about . . . Diaper Duty!

I love to feed the baby. It's not because I have to, but I just love it. I don't sleep much anyway, so if he cries, I'm up with the bottle. I do leave some of the diaper duties to my wife. She's much better at it! I think you should do the things you excel at in life.

Time-out

My advice for new moms is to take as much time off as you can at the beginning. That was the best advice I was given. Take the time because your child will never be that little again. I took six months with my son, Cal, and a year with Liv.

Another good bit of advice is to never use a diaper bag. You look like an idiot. You can take your big purse out and stick a few diapers in it. Don't carry that ugly diaper bag. Why look awful with this bottle stuck to the side of it? Get a cute purse and you'll feel so much better. I think diaper bags are a male conspiracy. They're horrible, horrible things.

— Julianne Moore

Will Ferrell

Daddy Dossier

International superstar Will Ferrell grew up in Orange County, California, where he wasn't sent to the principal's office all that often but did try out comedy routines on his fellow classmates. He graduated from the University of Southern California with a degree in sports broadcasting and then began performing with the Groundlings comedy troupe.

He spent time as a cast member on *Saturday Night Live,* where he made his mark impersonating George W. Bush. Will has also starred in hit movies including *Zoolander, Anchorman: The Legend of Ron Burgundy, Elf, Wedding Crashers, Talladega Nights: The Ballad of Ricky Bobby, Stranger Than Fiction,* and *Blades of Glory.* Will is married to Viveca Paulin; and they have a son, Magnus Paulin Ferrell, 3; and a baby boy, Mattia, who was born in December of 2006.

What I Know about . . .
Daddy Pampers

There are many parallels between my son and me. For instance, we both wear diapers. I started wearing a bladder-relief diaper just for convenience. I don't really have a problem, but I'm too lazy to go to the bathroom, and it just saves me a lot of time.

What I Know about . . .
Flying with Children

If you're flying with your children, it's best to book them on the same flight and not on one where they have more legroom and are leaving at a different time. They could get there earlier than you, and that causes resentment. Two-year-olds can also never figure out those connecting flights. It just makes it harder, so travel as a family.

What I Know about . . .
Embarrassing My Child (Imagine!)

In a general sense, I just commit to whatever I'm doing on-screen. Commitment in comedy is the biggest thing you have to do—regardless of whether it asks you to be in your underwear or not. I'll always just go for it. It's a shame if you don't commit with a whole heart to comedy, because what other pursuit gives you the license to do these things and not get arrested? You even get paid for it. I'm sure my teenage son will appreciate that paycheck when he's older even if Dad's in his underwear on the big screen.

Time-out

*I can be a strict father. The thing that gets my goat
is respect and decorum. If that's not there or you dis-
respect the family, then you're in big trouble with me.
I expect my children to have respect. But I also give
them the benefit of the doubt. I lead by example. I show
respect in my house and lead by a certain sense of decorum. You can't preach to a child. You gotta walk the talk.*

— Andy García

Bruce Willis

Daddy Dossier

Superstar Bruce Willis was born in Germany on a military base and grew up in Penns Grove, New Jersey. After graduating from high school, he attended Montclair State University in Montclair, New Jersey. He moved to New York to become an actor and was a bartender by night so that he could audition during the daylight hours. Pouring drinks paid off because a casting director wandered into his bar one night and gave him a small role in a movie as . . . a bartender.

Bruce's big break happened in 1985 when he became wisecracking detective David Addison on the popular ABC series *Moonlighting.* He crossed over to film with the hit *Die Hard* and then starred in *In Country, Die Hard 2, The Bonfire of the Vanities, Hudson Hawk, Pulp Fiction, Color of Night, Nobody's Fool, The Fifth Element, Armageddon, The Sixth Sense, Tears of the Sun, The Whole Ten Yards,* and *Sin City.*

He was married to Demi Moore from 1987 to 2000. They remain dedicated parents who live in mansions across the street from each other in Hailey, Idaho, where they raise their three children, Rumer Glenn, 17; Scout LaRue, 14; and Tallulah Belle, 11. They also have homes near each other in Los Angeles, where Demi lives with her new husband, Ashton Kutcher.

What I Know about . . .
Kids Changing Your Life

Before I had kids, I was just thinking about myself. It was just all me, my world, my needs. *Me, me, me. How am I going to get this? How am I going to get that? I want this. I want that.* And then I had my first daughter, Rumer. Oh, my God—it's unbelievable the change that came over me. Everything else seemed stupid once I had kids. Suddenly, I had this tiny little infant who needed all my help. I sat back and thought, *Who cares about the rest of it?*

What I Know about . . . Men and Children

I know that there are a lot of men out there who don't take care of the babies they bring into this world. That's a horrible situation. I can't imagine being that kind of man, and I don't get it. I'm much more proud of being a dad than anything else in my life, including being a movie star.

What I Know about . . .
Fatherhood after Divorce

We all get along, we're friends, and it works. I will take credit for living in a way that's best for my children. I think Demi and I have both chosen to rise above what you commonly see when parents separate. It was a pretty simple decision. We both love our kids and want to continue raising them together. If you just put the kids first, a lot of things come easily.

What I Know about . . . My Kids Dating

My girls know what those 14- and 16-year-old boys are thinking . . . because I told them. You've just got to talk honestly with them, sit them down, and say, "This is what's going on." No matter what these boys say, I tell them that girls have all the power.

Time-out

Now with our baby, Grace, we spell everything out in my house. We say, "She can't have a c-o-o-k-i-e." But later after Grace goes to bed, I'll say to my husband, Tim, "Do you want some i-c-e-c-r-e-a-m?" And the other day, I spelled out "d-a-n-m" after I burned myself on a pot. And my husband said, "Honey, you spelled that wrong." I yelled, "No, I didn't! Look it up!"

— **Elisabeth Hasselbeck,** cohost of *The View*

The Rock

Daddy Dossier

Dwayne "The Rock" Johnson grew up in Hawaii. His father, Rocky Johnson, and maternal grandfather were professional wrestlers. Dwayne nabbed a football scholarship at the University of Miami, but a back injury stopped him from joining the NFL. Instead, he went into the family business, becoming a professional wrestler called "The Rock" and a seven-time WWE champion.

The Rock eventually left the ring to try his luck at movies and has had roles in *The Mummy Returns* and *The Scorpion King;* and has starred in *The Rundown, Walking Tall, Be Cool, Doom,* and *Gridiron Gang.* He is married to Dany Johnson; and they have a daughter, Simone Alexandra, 5.

What I Know about . . .
Turning a Kid's Life Around

When I was a kid, we had no money. I came from a poor home. But still, I had love and a lot of support. Sadly, as a young teenager, I didn't pay attention to that love. When I was growing up in Hawaii, I did a lot of fighting . . . assault, theft, more fighting. I did a lot of things I shouldn't have been doing, and I made a lot of bad decisions. I hung around with the wrong people in a tough town where someone's mom would want to get in a fight with you.

But love got me through, and I was told to join a sports team, which really helped me. So I hope kids realize how lucky they are when their family loves them, and how far they can go, even if they mess up a bit. You can usually fix it. One way is to get involved with team sports, which becomes a second family to a lot of kids who are searching for love.

Now, I realize the importance of just having love at home and what that means. For parents, I say that even if the kid doesn't learn it right away and has to play catch-up, eventually the love that you teach that child at home will catch up to him or her like it did to me.

What I Know about . . .
Teaching My Daughter to Put Up Her Dukes

You want to teach your children how to handle themselves in any situation. It's inevitable that kids will get a little bit physical. Little girls get physical these days the same way that boys do.

What I do in my house is tell my baby girl, Simone, to talk to someone in charge if another kid is picking on her. I say, "What we do is communicate. Communication is key, honey. We talk things through. If there's a problem, go to the teacher and say, 'Listen I'm having a problem with Billy. He's doing such and such to me, and I don't like it.'" I tell her if the kid does it again, she goes right back to the teacher.

The other day, Simone said to me, "Well, Daddy what happens if he does it the third time?" I told her, "Then, honey, you take your right hand and push Billy as hard as you can in the face and pie-face [hit] him or slug him."

That's when my wife got involved and said, "Dwayne! Are you teaching our baby to fight?" I said, "Honey, I'm kidding! I'm kidding! But, Simone, first you put up your right fist. . . ."

Babies are amazing: the way they stare into your eyes; their exuberant smiles; how they begin each day all warm and sleeping, smelling of promise. I suppose I never realized it before, but babies aren't really born of their parents. They're born of every kind word, loving gesture, hope, and dream their parents ever had. Bliss.

— **Julia Roberts** on being the mommy
of twins Phinnaeus (aka Finn) and Hazel

Faith Hill

Mommy Material

Faith Hill is a native of Star, Mississippi. She began her career at age two, because as soon as she could speak, she began to sing. Church solos led to singing in prisons and at rodeos, fairs, and local events.

At age 19, she moved to Nashville to work as an assistant to Reba McEntire. After years spent pounding the pavement, she released her multiplatinum debut, *Take Me as I Am,* in 1993. Other multiplatinum CDs include 1995's *It Matters to Me* and 1998's *Faith.* She crossed over to the pop charts with the hit 2002 CD *Cry.*

Faith made her film debut in a remake of *The Stepford Wives.* She has sold 30 million albums and has received countless honors and accolades, including four Grammy® wins, three awards from the Country Music Association, and 12 statues from the Academy of Country Music. Her sixth CD, *Fireflies,* debuted at number one on both the country- and pop-album charts in 2005.

Faith is married to country crooner Tim McGraw; and they have three children together, Gracie Katherine, 9; Maggie Elizabeth, 8; and Audrey Caroline, 5.

What I Know about . . .
Looking Fancy in Front of My Kids

Not so long ago, I was doing *Oprah* and flew back home in time to pick up my girls from school. Usually I get them with absolutely no makeup on and my hair in a messy ponytail. So I pick them up after coming home from *Oprah,* and they give me "the look." They're so embarrassed. *Mortified.* Why does Mom have to look so fancy (as if this was the most terrible thing on Earth)?

You see, my children don't parade me around as Faith Hill, the singer. They're just like any other kids. They don't care if you're a fancy doctor or a big-time businesswoman. They just want Mom.

So the day when I came home from *Oprah,* the kids were like, "Mooooommmmmm, get back in the car. Immediately! Why are you wearing all that makeup? Why is your hair down? It's so fluffy! We don't like it fluffy! You're embarrassing us!" I guess the moral of the story is that they want you to do one thing: Fit in with the other moms, or else!

What I Know about . . . Time Pressure and Stress When It Comes to Young-uns

There's no secret when it comes to juggling this career and motherhood. At the end of the day, I just throw my feet up on the couch and say, "God, that was a long day! But somehow it all worked."

There are days when everyone is fussy, fighting, and late. Gracie has long hair, and sometimes it's such a fight to brush it in the morning and get her ready for school. But I think about the days when she'll be too big and tall. She won't ever let me brush her hair then, so I enjoy the little moments now even if they're not perfect.

Time-Out

My son has a dream book. I got him a blank book years ago and one for myself. We drew in them until 4 in the morning the first night. Of course, he filled his up in an hour. It's amazing that I only got five pages in to mine. That's a tribute to the imagination of children. You just have to give them a blank page and let them go. . . . I decided to use my journal for them. I write down all the funny stuff they do and say. When they get older, I'll give it to them so they can remember their own childhood.

— **Robert Rodriguez,** film director whose credits include *Spy Kids* and *The Adventures of Shark Boy and Lavagirl in 3-D;* the father of five children: four boys, Rocket, Racer, Rebel, and Rogue; and one girl, Rhiannon

Tim McGraw

Daddy Dossier

Cowboy-hat-wearing, *GQ*-handsome country superstar Tim McGraw grew up in Louisiana. His father was baseball player Tug McGraw, a star relief pitcher for the New York Mets. Tim attended the University of Louisiana at Monroe on a baseball scholarship with plans to study sports medicine. He began to play guitar and sing on the local club circuit, eventually moving to Nashville, where he nabbed his first record deal.

Tim has six multiplatinum CDs and a slew of hit singles. He also fell in love with his opening act, the gorgeous Faith Hill, who later became his wife. Recently, Tim has been expanding his horizons and has had roles in such films as *Friday Night Lights* and *Flicka.* He has three daughters with Faith—Gracie, Maggie, and Audrey.

What I Know about . . . Raising Baby Girls

I have to say that my first bit of advice about raising daughters is that you should consider yourself very lucky. I know that I'll be well taken care of when I'm an old, old, old man. Just the other day, the girls wouldn't let me out of the house. They said, "Daddy, you're not wearing that!" It's not like I was in clown pants—I was wearing khakis and a nice shirt. One of my daughters just stood there shaking her head. Finally, she said, "You look too much like a dad. Go and put on your jeans."

That's a funny story . . . but I'm a very serious parent. I think you have to be a little strict, especially having girls. You can't be their friend, because you're their parent. I'm especially strict about homework. I throw the hammer down. No friends. No talking on the phone. No TV. You gotta do your homework before you start doing the fun stuff.

What I Know about . . . Co-parenting

Faith and I do the team thing with the kids. We back one another up each and every time because this is crucial. You must support the other adult in the house with the kids—even if you know the other adult is wrong. You need to remain on the same page, because if you're not together each time, then all hell will break loose.

What I Know about . . . Being the Only Guy in a Home Full of Women

In my case, I live in a household of all women, as fathers do. I've learned that the best thing I can do under those circumstances is to just shut up. I never win anyway. I don't even *try* to win anymore. If I can break even, then I'm doing all right. I'm all about give-and-take, I guess. The problem is that when you live in a house that's all women, everyone has their "take," and the poor guy just has to shut up!

What I Know about . . . Daddies and Girls

I like to kid around, but it's just amazing to raise three daughters. You want to protect them, and honestly, you never want them to leave home. It's different with boys. You want your sons to do well, go out there, get jobs, and leave home. It's about the push for the future. The girls just hit you in the heart. You don't care if they ever get a job and leave home. Hell, they could get married and move back in with you, and then everyone could just live under the same roof! The other day, one of my girls told Faith and me that they weren't moving out until they were 35. We couldn't help smiling at each other because this sounded real good to us.

What I Know about . . . Guilt

I suppose all parents think that they're doing a bad job. I haven't met a parent yet who thinks he or she is dead-on, but what I've learned is that there's no blanket way to do it. Every kid is different, and they all have to be handled differently. You shouldn't feel guilty about doing your best with each individual child, because that's all you can do.

What I Know about . . . My Daughters Dating

Oh, my girls aren't dating—until I'm dead. There's no such thing as a nice guy. I was a clean-cut, so-called nice guy . . . and I wasn't that nice!

We went on a vacation to this luxury resort where the idea was that the kids and my wife would be in the pool and I'd get to play golf. One morning, my golf partner canceled, but I still went to the driving range to hit a few balls. When I came back to have lunch, I found my entire family at the pool and walked over to join them. One of my sons looked up from his raft in the extremely crowded pool, and at the top of his lungs, screamed, "Oh, there's my dad. And he spent the entire morning playing with himself!"

— **Ray Romano** on the humiliation factor involved in parenting

Denzel Washington

Daddy Dossier

A Mount Vernon, New York, native, Denzel Washington is one of three children, the son of a Pentecostal minister and a beautician. Denzel once planned on becoming a journalist and studied writing at Fordham University. A turn in a school play changed his life, and he wound up at the American Conservatory Theater (A.C.T.) studying theater.

Denzel quickly found work playing Dr. Philip Chandler on the hit TV series *St. Elsewhere.* He went on to star in a slew of films, including *A Soldier's Story, Cry Freedom, Mo' Better Blues, Malcolm X, Philadelphia, Crimson Tide, Courage Under Fire, Remember the Titans, Training Day,* and *American Gangster.* He also directed the award-winning *Antwone Fisher.*

Denzel and his wife, Pauletta, are the parents of four children: John David, 23; Katia, 21; and twins Malcolm and Olivia, 15.

What I Know about . . .
Being a Disciplinarian Dad

My kids get away with things? Are you kidding me? I'm the dad who's always on the road on a film set. My biggest thing is learning how not to feel guilty about being away. And therefore, part of getting over my guilt is letting them get away with murder. But let's get real. I can't walk in after being gone for six weeks and become Disciplinarian Dad who's barking, "Did you do your homework?" I'd expect my kid to say, "Who are you? You've been gone for a month." It's the same for any parent who travels. You have to cool it. The key for me is to blend back into family life when I come home.

What I Know about . . . Bonding

I got an earring when my son turned 16. We went together—it seemed like a cool father-son thing to do. Of course, this is an individual parental decision.

What I Know about . . .
Giving Other Parents Advice

My best advice to parents? Just stick with your kids. There's no set of rules on how to be a parent. No handbook. Just hang around your kids and ask them a lot of questions.

What I Know about . . .
Raising Healthy Kids in Troubling Times

My youngest daughter will use the catchphrase: "I need my space." There's no space in my house. I'm not trying to frighten her, but I'm concerned about our high-tech world. She's on the Internet, and that's not something to be taken lightly. There are predators out there. You have to stay involved in your children's lives and monitor everything they're doing whether they like it or not. You're not in the job of making them like it. You're there to protect them in a world that can be troubling.

What I Know about . . . Children and Luck

I was watching *Geraldo.* I watched it the other night, and someone said something that was very enlightening about life as a parent: "It's really 50 percent luck." That makes sense to me.

Time-out

*I have a one-year-old. I think having a stroller in
New York is harder than starring on Broadway.
Oh, man! Everyone is just so aggressive. They would
rather walk into you and your child. I just wish people
could give parents a little consideration. Plus, for the
life of me I can't put that Bugaboo stroller together.*

— Dylan McDermott

Vickie Chachere

Mommy Material

Vickie Chachere is an editorial writer for *The Tampa Tribune* and has been a journalist in Florida for 17 years, covering law and order; politics; and major new stories such as the 2000 Presidential-election recount, the battle over Terri Schiavo, and numerous hurricanes.

She is a native of Applegate, Oregon, and a graduate of Arizona State University. Vickie is married to journalist Doug Stanley, and they're the parents of two children, Taylor, 17; and Nicholas, 4.

What I Know about . . .
Mixing Work with Motherhood

What I know about juggling work and motherhood is to not let either become overwhelming. It's easier said than done . . . it's almost impossible to do both perfectly and still be human. There are days you can do one very well and days you'll do neither well—but those days end. The only thing you can do is enjoy the journey, because the years your children are young are fleeting, and it's not worth spending them miserably counting all the things you aren't accomplishing instead of celebrating your achievements.

If you work outside of the home as I do, you do it either because your family needs you to or because you have a job that's your calling. The hardest adjustment I had to make when I went back to work after nearly a year of maternity leave was to free myself from the guilt of wanting to work. I was one of the lucky few who had exactly the kind of career I'd planned for myself, but I didn't want to spend my life doing just journalism. I was fortunate that at the time, I worked for the Associated Press, which offered long maternity leaves, so when Nicholas came along, I could take time off and enjoy motherhood.

Hands down, that was the most wonderful year of my life. I did nothing but concentrate on my baby, love him, and nurture him. It was simply a magical time. But like in most families, living on one income isn't possible in this economy, and after nearly a year, it was time for me to go back to work. And I was ready. Staying at home with a baby, while wonderful, is also isolating. If you have the kind of personality that's drawn to the news business to start with, you crave being in the thick of things.

I had no clue what I was doing when I tried to balance my career and family, and the truth is that there are some days when I still don't. But I made myself a promise when I went back to work: I was going to knock myself out while I was there, but I was going to draw a line between my business life and my family life, and I wouldn't apologize for it.

When working full-time was too hard, I asked my boss to give me a 32-hour week. Any new working mom will tell you that the first months your children are in day care, they pick up tons of germs. I missed a lot of work with a sick kid, reasoning that if Nick spent less time at day care and had a break in the middle of the week, he'd be healthier. I was right.

The new schedule gave us a day to decompress in the middle of the week, and we were both healthier because of it. So many moms never ask for any concessions at work because they fear it will look as if they're asking for favors. Well, so what if it does? If your boss is happy to grant some leeway, take it.

Eventually, though, it was time for the full 40-hour week and a new job as an editorial writer. The reality is, nearly every day feels like you're a salmon swimming upstream all the time. It's exhausting, it's overwhelming, and you're racked with guilt (actually the fish are lucky—they don't feel guilty).

Here's the crazy thing: A good friend of mine who's brilliant and accomplished stays home with her three beautiful children—and *she* feels guilty. She worries about having set aside her career and becoming one-dimensional, and she fears that her daughters won't believe her when she says it's important that they get an education and build careers for themselves. She feels guilty for being overwhelmed by them and wanting time to herself.

The guilt is going to be there whether you work or stay home, so you might as well pick the path that feels best to you. The goal here is to raise happy, healthy, well-adjusted children . . . and to enjoy the ride.

So this is what I've learned to do along the way:

— What your kids want most when you're home with them, morning and evening, is *you.* Mornings are crazy, so do what you can the night before to make them easier. Evenings I spend playing, snuggling, and learning about Nicholas's day. It's the best part of our time together hearing the new song he learned in school or having him tell me about the game he and his buddies made up on the playground.

— Don't spend your days and nights making lists of things to do; instead, focus on what you've accomplished. It's easy to come home and see the toys cluttering the living room and the dishes in the sink and beat yourself up because your home isn't spotless. Unless you're hosting tea parties in the middle of the week, who are you really trying to impress? It's far better to ignore the mess and spend your evenings reconnecting with your children than obsessing over whether the floors need mopping. You don't want the health department knocking on your door, but if your house doesn't look camera-ready for *Martha Stewart Living,* it isn't a crime.

— Pick your perfection. Everyone has the measure that represents his or her standard of living. For me, it's dinner. To me, quality of life means a home-cooked meal on the table and dinner together. We rarely eat takeout or go out in the middle of the week, and I've never served a frozen dinner. I cook food that can be reheated on Sunday or use a Crock-Pot during the day. It's more work than going to a drive-through, but I've picked my battle, and this is it. To me, having a good, healthy meal means our lives haven't been overtaken by work.

For someone else, it might be a clean house, being the star volunteer at school, or an impeccable yard. Whatever the standard is, allow yourself one, but don't feel like you've got to do everything perfectly.

— Reward yourself and your family for a job well done. I don't feel bad about spending some of my hard-earned money on myself or indulging my child or husband. I work darn hard for that money, and at the end of the week, we deserve a little treat for having made it through. I want Nicholas to understand that there are rewards for hard work, and it's not just work for work's sake.

On Saturdays, my husband takes some time to play golf, and Nicholas and I have a standing lunch date. As we run our errands, I let him pick out a little trinket. So he has more action figures than he needs? But then we come home and play with them together.

The strangest thing I hear from working moms is even more guilt for using some of their earnings for little luxuries—as if somehow the money must always be used to pay bills, otherwise the time they spend earning it is frivolous. That's nonsense. You should enjoy the fruits of your labor.

Nicholas understands, too, that I do appreciate the effort he makes each week. It's no small task getting yourself out the door when you really want to hang out for one more episode of *Go, Diego, Go!*

— Learn to let it go. I think back to one day when Nicholas was about a year old and I'd spent the entire day putting out fires before I scrambled to get him from day care. I was talking to my editor on the telephone as we headed home in maddening traffic. I swear, the exact moment I said, "I don't think anything more can go wrong today!" was when Nicholas threw up all over the backseat. And you know what? Even that mess got cleaned up.

These are the nutty years. I've come to accept that it may be some time before I feel that I'm doing enough at work or enough at home. I'm not going to go to the gym as much as I want. I'm not going to get all the errands done, and my flower beds are full of weeds—but you know what? That's okay. I've got the happiest, healthiest little boy I could have ever imagined, and every day that I get to see him grow into this incredible person is a blessing.

When he's grown and I look back on this time, I'm not going to remember that it takes me two weeks to pick up the dry cleaning, or that my rosebushes died because I never got around to spraying them, or that the toilet needed scrubbing, or that my desk was a mess, or that I never got around to cleaning out my e-mail in-box, so the tech guys had to do it for me. I'm going to remember the evening last week when I sat on the bathroom rug while Nicholas took a bath and recited a long poem he'd memorized at school, and that later he cuddled up against me for story time before he fell asleep. I'll remember that evening a few weeks ago when he was sitting on my lap and reached up, patted my cheek, and nonchalantly said, "I'm lucky you're my mom." And all I could think was: *No, I'm the lucky one.*

Time-out

*What I tell my friends who don't have
kids is: "Embrace your boredom! Because
when you have children, it's gone."*

— **Edward Burns,** actor and director whose credits
include *She's the One* and *The Brothers McMullen*

Hugh Jackman

Daddy Dossier

Aussie native Hugh Jackman is the youngest of five children who grew up with British parents. He studied drama at Western Australian Academy of Performing Arts and got his start on the Australian TV series *Correlli,* where he met his future wife, the lovely actress Deborra-Lee Furness.

Hugh has received rave reviews for his stage work in *Sunset Boulevard, Oklahoma!,* and *The Boy from Oz.* On the big screen, he's starred in *Swordfish, Kate & Leopold, Van Helsing, Scoop, The Fountain, The Prestige,* and *Flushed Away.* He plays tough but furry Wolverine in the *X-Men* franchise and will do a solo turn as the carnivore in *Wolverine.*

Hugh and Deborra-Lee have two adopted children, Oscar Maximillian, 6; and Ava Eliot, 1.

What I Know about . . .
Taking Kids Out in Public

I never get embarrassed when children act out in public. You really have to leave that at the door and just go with what happens.

I can tell you a quick story. I took my son, Oscar, to one of the art museums in New York City. He was three, and we were in the Impressionists' room. Oscar was pointing and laughing at the paintings. You've never seen a human being on this earth who was more full of joy. That's when this woman came up to me and said in a very huffy voice, "Will you please keep that child of yours quiet? You're in a museum!"

I said, "Absolutely not. I will not keep him quiet, because he's three. He's also getting more enjoyment out of these paintings than you are, ma'am. So maybe it's you who should learn a lesson here!"

What I Know about . . . Boys vs. Girls

It's so different being the father of a little girl versus being the father of a boy. I'm a little more relaxed with Oscar because he's a boy. I'm a guy, and I know what he'll go through at school and with girls. I know he'll be tough like his father. But with my daughter, who's only ten months old, I just hold her and think, *I don't want you to face anything bad ever in your life. You're a sweet little girl.*

I know that's old-fashioned thinking, but ask any man. We just can't help being overly protective of our daughters. I think it's only natural, and no one can talk us out of it. That said, I do want to mention that both of my children are wonderful, and I'm so blessed.

What I Know about . . .
Raising Normal Children

We've opted to live in New York City. In Los Angeles, it would be a big burden for my kids to be the son and daughter of Wolverine from the *X-Men* movies. It would be all about "My dad is so-and-so, and your dad is Wolverine."

It's so funny. My father was an accountant, and I thought the fax machine in his office was the coolest thing in the world, although the other kids at my school couldn't have cared less. But I still had a normalcy that my kids won't have, and that's a little bit upsetting to me. For all of those parents in very normal jobs, your children will thank you for it.

What I Know about . . . Supernanny!

My wife and I sit around and watch *Supernanny.* I'm not kidding. She's so good, and she actually taught us how to get our kids to go to sleep. The deal is, you put the children in their cot [crib], sit next to it, and don't look at them . . . you must be boring—at least that's what "Supernanny" says to do and be. Remember that if your kids get out of bed again and are fussy about going to sleep, take them by the hand and bring them back to bed. Don't look at them. Every two minutes, move a little closer to the door of their room until you're out the door and they're hopefully sleeping in their cots—their own cots! There will be no sleeping in your bed . . . Supernanny will be mad at you!

Honestly, this sleep technique works. The children might be a bit pissed off at first, but they're just mad. They aren't afraid, which is key. I did this, and within three days, my daughter was sleeping through the night and waking up happy. But my son never got it right because we didn't have Supernanny back when he was young, and we took everyone else's bad advice!

What I Know about . . . Halloween

Oscar loves my character, Wolverine, from *X-Men*. He got dressed up as Wolverine for Halloween a few years ago. He loved it. He'd knock on a door and say, "Trick or treat—I'll slice you in half!" Not knowing the rules of Halloween, my son would just walk into the houses. He'd go upstairs or right to the back, and I'd say, "Excuse me. This is because we've moved so many times." I said to my wife, Deb, "We've got to stop moving around. We go trick-or-treating and our son thinks we've moved. It's frightening."

What's almost funny for me was that when I went with Oscar, I actually wore my claws from *X-Men.* I had the claws on my hands when people would open the door, and 50 houses later no one had noticed it was me—not one person. Finally, someone said, "You're that guy." So now we're moving to that street . . . just kidding.

Time-out

*Every time I do something bad,
I just say to my kids, "Save it for the book."*

— **Rosie O'Donnell**

Kate Hudson

Mommy Material

The daughter of screen legend Goldie Hawn and singer Bill Hudson, and the stepdaughter of actor Kurt Russell, Kate Hudson grew up loving to act. In fact, Goldie says, "She was always singing and dancing around the house. I knew that she was born to become an actress."

Kate began her career with a small role on the acclaimed TV show *Party of Five.* Her early movies include *200 Cigarettes, About Adam,* and *Gossip;* and she was nominated for an Oscar for playing cute groupie Penny Lane in Cameron Crowe's hit film *Almost Famous.* Kate went on to become a young A-list star, with roles in *The Four Feathers; How to Lose a Guy in 10 Days; Alex & Emma; Le Divorce; Raising Helen; The Skeleton Key;* and *You, Me and Dupree.*

Kate has a three-year-old son, Ryder, whom she insists "is the love of my life."

What I Know about . . .
My Child's Imagination

My son is two, and he's talking up a storm. It's amazing that at this age he's starting to create his own ideas along with the words. Ryder is obsessed with Peter Pan right now. He'll watch the DVD and then actually use Peter Pan in his real life.

The other day my girlfriend was over and we were chatting. Ryder walked up to us and said, "Girls, you talk too much." We were shocked and laughed. Then it dawned on me that this was the exact line Peter Pan said to Wendy. Ryder picked right up on it, as all children do.

Meanwhile, I thought, *You're only two and a half, and damn if being with you every single day isn't just what life is about right now.* That's the reason to live. I'm watching him discover every part of himself. His mind is just fantastic.

What I Know about . . .
Taking Time for Yourself

I can't stand it when people give me parenting advice. I'm like, "Would everybody please stop with the advice. Shut up!" But my advice if someone asked me is simple: Make sure to take a little bit of time for yourself every day. Even if you have to lock yourself in the bathroom for two minutes to just twiddle your thumbs, do it. I feel like it's our nature as women to take care of everything and be totally consumed. It's so easy for us to forget about ourselves. It's important to be present and strong for your kids and know that you really need some breathing space.

Time-out

Don't try to do it all by yourself. You need to ask your husband and your family for help. That doesn't make you a bad mother. You have to admit that you can't do every single thing. Two children are a lot to handle. Other than that, all I can say about twins is that they'll always compare themselves to each other. Make sure that as their mother you give each one an equal amount of love and attention.

— **Jane Seymour** on raising twins
Kristopher and John, born in 1995

The best way to approach bathing, feeding, and dressing is like an assembly line: Have all the items you need ready to use before you start.

— **Joan Lunden,** broadcaster,
former *Good Morning America* host, and
mother of two sets of twins via a surrogate

Ashton Kutcher

Stepdaddy Dossier

Iowa native Ashton Kutcher starred on the hit Fox TV series *That '70s Show* and also created and starred in MTV's raucous prank show *Punk'd.* He made the leap to the big screen with the remake *Guess Who,* along with the action flick *The Guardian,* the romantic comedy *A Lot Like Love,* and the animated film *Open Season.*

He's married to actress Demi Moore and is the stepfather of her three daughters, Rumer, Scout, and Tallulah.

What I Know about . . . Being a Stepparent

I like being what the girls call MOD—"my other Dad." What I've learned in the last year is that every kid is different. But as long as you love them and never forget that love, then you have the key. I think it's all about just being there and loving them because kids feel that every single day.

What I Know about . . .
Being the Homework Heavyweight

I think part of your job as a parent is to support your kids in whatever they need. If they need help with the homework, then I'm there. If they have an interest, I want to help them explore it. That's being a good parent. I'm learning as I grow and doing the best I can. You support their vision and help their dreams come true. You enable them to fly.

Am I strict? Nah. They're really responsible kids. They do a really good job. I don't really think our parenting situation is much different from anyone else's out there.

What I Know about . . . Love

I've definitely taught the girls how to give really good hugs. It's the most important thing.

I used to hear the song that talks about
believing the children are our future and think it
was a trite song. Now I realize it's a warning.

— Jon Stewart

Adam Sandler

Daddy Dossier

Adam Sandler is a New York native and one of the funniest big-screen comedians of his generation. He's starred in films such as *The Waterboy, Happy Gilmore, Big Daddy,* and *Click,* in addition to doing a stint on *Saturday Night Live.*

Along with his wife, Jackie, he's a proud parent to baby Sadie Madison. He's not sure if he wants Sadie listening to his comedy recordings or watching any of his movies, either—at least not for the next decade or so. "I don't want my kid to hear any of the albums I made for now. I don't know what I'll do when she gets older. I hope she enjoys the movies I made, but she probably won't dig them until she's 14. I know I'll be like, 'Honey, let's watch Daddy again in *The Waterboy.*'"

What I Know about . . . Moral Support

I see the actual diapers go on, and I cheer my wife for doing such a good job. I'll also say, "Honey, good feeding! Way to go! Nice milk!"

What I Know about . . . Feeding the Baby

Every day I feel more comfortable with the baby. The only thing is, I want the baby to feel comfortable with me. I'm klutzy. It's like my arms aren't long enough.

What I Know about . . . the Baby Changing Your Life

I knew I'd be excited. I was dying to be a father. I didn't realize that it would be so much fun to have a baby in the house. But it's surprising how the baby looks through me. Every time I think the kid really likes me—and that she's staring into my eyes with love— I realize that she's just looking at my forehead. She's staring at a zit on my face.

What I Know about . . . the Future

When she dates, it will be ugly. I will not encourage dating. I'll get my friends Rob Schneider and David Spade to come over to rough up the boys who want to take her out.

Melissa says, "Mother, you criticize me!" I say, "No I don't. That's the stupidest thing you've ever said!"

— **Joan Rivers,** the nonjudgmental mother of Melissa Rivers

Michele Shapiro

Mommy Material

Michele Shapiro is the entertainment director at *Self* magazine. She's also worked as an editor at publications such as *Glamour, Seventeen,* and *Time Out New York.*

Michele lives with her husband and seven-year-old daughter, Esme, in New York City; and she's proud to juggle a career and motherhood on a daily basis.

What I Know about . . .
Getting Ready for School

For a long time, my seven-year-old daughter, Esme, was the biggest procrastinator when it came to getting ready for school. I'd wake her up in the morning and say, "Time to get ready. Let's start by brushing your teeth." Of course, I'd hear, "In a minute, Mommy!" Then her head would hit the pillow again.

So I bought an old-fashioned egg timer. I'd say, "You have 15 minutes to get ready for school, honey." I'd even give her a list of what she needed to do: "Get dressed, brush your teeth, and come to breakfast." At the end of the 15 minutes, the timer would go off, and she was supposed to be at our kitchen table at breakfast.

The timer had a great effect. The minute I'd wind it, my daughter would spring out of bed and move into immediate action. Then a funny thing happened: She started to really hate the timer. I'd walk into her room with it, and she'd say, "Mommy, please don't set the timer. I'll just get up and get going." I love how this worked, and the procrastination just went out the window.

This works great with kids, because just telling them they have 15 minutes to get ready really means nothing to a small child. They can't judge what 15 minutes really means in their minds. But the timer is something else—they watch the minutes go by and they want to please you. So they're at the sink brushing their teeth and watching the time in the same way an adult watches the clock in the morning. (By the way, a school psychologist suggested this one to me and many other parents, and we're grateful because it really works.)

What I Know about . . . Homework

Esme just started to bring home schoolwork. It's a struggle for parents of young children to figure out how to work this into their home life. What I find is that my daughter will come home from school tired. She'll immediately want to turn on the TV or the computer and just relax. With the homework looming, I have to be really firm about her not relaxing until she finishes everything. This means no TV, no computer, and no playing until she gets the work done.

It also helps that I bought her a desk where she can do her work. It's her own special place to concentrate. When I was little, I didn't have a desk and always did my homework on a coffee table or at the kitchen table. I thought it was really important that as soon as Esme started kindergarten she had her own desk in her bedroom, which is a nice, quiet place to do her homework. Of course, that desk is piled up now, and you can barely find anyplace to write. But it's her mess, and she finds the space to do her work in privacy. That's a good life habit to learn.

What I Know about . . .
Sharing Parenting Tasks with My Husband

Something that most couples eventually run into is dealing with different parenting styles. My husband and I were brought up differently, and it follows that we have varying ideas about raising children. Our philosophies are not the same in this area, which can lead to problems. For example, my husband's family is much more strict and matter-of-fact. I'm all about the love and the support. My parents are very supportive types of people.

It's really important when you come together as new parents to try to get on the same page—especially if you come from different backgrounds. At least you must meet in the middle and arrive at agreements so the child isn't getting mixed messages and playing one parent off the other. My daughter is extremely strong-willed, which is a trait that I love in her. She has strong opinions, which is fantastic but challenging. It's important that my husband and I agree on how to parent this type of child.

Take our rule about homework. My husband and I agree that there's no TV or going on the computer until the homework is done. My daughter can come to my husband or me. She can appeal and ask if this rule can change, but we'll never bend, because we're on the same page with each other and our daughter. We've also agreed that she can only watch TV for an hour after everything that needs to be done is done. The TV viewing is used as a reward.

What I Know about . . . Setting Limits

You have to set limits, and the truth is, kids like them as much as they complain about them. Of course your kids will push the limits—that's expected, and you also did this as a child. If your kids didn't, then they would be "Stepford" children. They're always testing how far they can push it.

For example, my daughter is a huge *Project Runway* fan. Sadly, it's on at 10 P.M. on Wednesday in New York City, where we live. Each week on those Wednesday nights, I'll hear little footsteps coming out of Esme's bedroom at 10 P.M.—she's trying to hear what's happening on her favorite show.

It's not that I'm against the show. Esme has become a little designer because of it and has an entire spring collection she made out of garbage bags. I actually once showed them to Heidi Klum, who was doing an interview with the magazine, and she said, "We should do *Project Runway* for kids."

Anyway, we record the original show at home so my daughter can watch it the next day. Then we make her get back in bed when we hear her tiptoeing out of her room, because it's the rule. It's so hard to be strict when you know your child loves something. I hate to deny her, but you must have rules.

What I Know about . . .
Putting Your Child on a Schedule

I believe that kids need to be on a schedule. You can't let them just do anything they want at any time, day or night. The truth of the matter is that a schedule is a security blanket for kids. They want and need to have structured lives. When you let it all go and adopt an "Anything goes because it's fun" way of life, then the children suffer. If you let them stay up as late as they want, they'll suffer in school the next day.

My daughter wants to stay up late, so I'm always telling her, "You really need your sleep, and so do Mom and Dad. It's very important for your body and your brain." I know she's a different child when she goes to bed at 8:30 versus 10:30. She has so much more energy when she gets a good night's sleep.

What I Know about . . . Raising a Night Owl

My daughter is a born night owl. Both my husband and I are late-night people, and Esme wants to be awake with us because she loves to stay up and then sleep in. I talk to my friends and know that most kids get up at 6 in the morning, while my daughter can easily sleep until 10. So this is always a challenge for us, and I know there are many parents who go through the same struggle.

At our house, it can be tough to just get Esme into bed. But one thing I found that works great is a CD sent to me by a record company called Liquid Music. It's made for falling asleep, and it really works. I put it in her little CD player in her room, and ten minutes later she's out for the night.

I also took my daughter to a "Yoga for Kids" class. Those are great for children who have trouble sleeping because they teach them how to relax their body and mind. There are other nights without the music when I'll say to my daughter, "Remember our yoga class. Do your deep-belly breathing and close your eyes." Once again, ten minutes later she's out for the night. Thank you, yoga.

*I'm the everyday nag. I think kids feel good
when they know that you're watching them.
If you said nothing, they wouldn't feel secure.*

— Susan Sarandon

Tina Fey

Mommy Material

Tina Fey writes, executive-produces, and stars as Liz Lemon on NBC's *30 Rock.* She grew up in Upper Darby Township, Pennsylvania, and later studied drama at the University of Virginia.

After graduation, Tina worked at the YMCA in Chicago while training at Second City to learn improv comedy. She sent a packet of sketches to Lorne Michaels of *Saturday Night Live* and received a job offer a week later at Studio 8H. She became the first female head writer of the show. She also co-anchored *Weekend Update* with Amy Poehler.

Tina raises her one-year-old daughter, Alice, with her husband, Jeff Richmond.

What I Know about . . .
Children's Birthday Parties

My daughter is delightful. She's the love of my life. In fact, she just turned one, and we had a small family birthday party for her because they say, "Don't overwhelm the baby." Okay, the truth is, I rented out the club Butter, and we had 1,000 people. I'm just kidding, because the truth is, some parents go nuts with these parties. It's better to keep it simple or you really do overwhelm children and they don't have any fun.

What I Know about . . .
Being a Working Mom

Every working mom feels that it's impossible. You get up and think, *This is another day, and it really is impossible.* But you keep going, and the next day you keep going. You do the impossible and juggle it all. Having a kid is an instant priority adjustment, but somehow everyone gets the day done.

Time-out

*If the boys come to the door with my daughter,
I say, "Whatever you do to her tonight, I'm
going to do to you when you bring her home."
That sounds like good teen parenting to me.*

— Sean Penn

Jon Secada

Daddy Dossier

Jon Secada came to the U.S. at age nine from Cuba and began his new life in Miami, where his family opened a coffee shop. At the University of Miami, he earned B.A. and M.A. degrees in jazz vocals. He cowrote songs for Gloria Estefan and was a backup singer on her tour.

Jon began his solo career in 1992 and quickly ascended to the top of the adult contemporary charts. He has sold six million records and played to sold-out crowds. His album *Otro Día Más Sin Verte* became the number one Latin album in 1992 and won a Grammy for Best Latin Pop Album. His CD *Heart, Soul, and a Voice* sold more than a million copies in 1994. He has also written songs for Ricky Martin and Jennifer Lopez.

Jon is the proud pop of two children.

What I Know about . . .
Making the Time for Parenting

Parenting has been an enlightening experience. I have two kids, who are seven and three. Directly or indirectly, consciously or unconsciously, they've changed my entire life and my focus. The trickiest part of this change is to make the time for the kids, which is an ongoing battle because my career as a singer means I'm traveling. I'm not unlike any other parent who's forced to lead a hectic life because of the job. I think the key is that you must communicate every single day with your child. No matter how long you're gone, you can't miss a day. Just be in touch. You don't want to lose one 24-hour period.

You need to stay tuned in to what your child is thinking about or feeling on that day. You must remain a part of their lives on a daily basis even if you can't be there. I know other parents might think, *So what if I miss a day? I'll be home tomorrow.* It's not good enough. Perhaps there was a fight at school or another kid was mean to your child. Your child is struggling through those life episodes, and he or she can't wait until tomorrow for your guidance and love.

What I Know about . . . Patience

If I've learned anything, it's that parenting requires supreme patience. Even when you're tired or your children are whining or cranky, you have to make them the focus of your attention. Children need to know that you're there for them even when they're not at their best. They need to know that you're not going anywhere. Your attention means love to them. Your communication with them shows them that no matter what, you still care about them. Helping your kids during times that aren't so easy actually draws you closer to them.

What I Know about . . . Discipline

As for moments when discipline is required . . . well, I have to admit that mostly it's my wife on the discipline. When I'm home, I do my share. We do time-outs followed by "I love you." Those work great, especially if you mean it and do it. You also must explain to the child the exact reason for the time-out. It can't be: "You're driving me crazy." It has to be a reason such as: "I told you to stop hitting your sister." Your children will learn this way which behaviors are acceptable and which aren't good. They'll also come to realize that certain acts will create a problem for them—that is, the time-out. Believe me, kids don't want those time-outs, so they'll eventually stop the act that caused them the problem in the first place.

What I Know about . . . Raising a Little Boy

It's funny, but boys and girls are truly different creatures. My boy has major energy, and his attention span is different. My daughter is calmer—my boy is a handful. His attention span doesn't give him the freedom to be into anything longer than five minutes. I've found that a schedule and outside activities are even more important with a boy. We have him in sports and gymnastics. My daughter is more content to play by herself or sing.

What I Know about . . . Encouraging Your Child's Natural Talents

By the way, my daughter has an amazing voice. If she ever wants to use it and follow in my footsteps— well, I better stop here, because of course she can do anything that makes her happy. But she has this natural voice. I don't go out of my way to talk about singing with her. We just play around and sing songs around the house. It's nothing conscious, because I don't want this to become a chore for her. I let her watch me play my music if she wants to, and if she doesn't, then she can go play with her toys. She comes to my shows with her mom, and I sing to her at night. Maybe someday she can be my opening act . . . or older Daddy will be *her* opening act! Well, I better stop now!

Time-out

We grew up with spankings in the ghetto. We had hand-me-downs that were ragged, but when your cousin got a torn pair of old blue jeans, you still said to the adult, "Oh, so you like him better." My grandparents did spankings . . . the neighbors spanked you! We were afraid of the schoolteachers, too. We'd go to class in the morning, look at our teacher, and say, "Is she calm?"

What does this have to do with how I parented? Well, I didn't do any of the above. I stayed on top of my children, but I did it through rewarding them for their good deeds. I think the generation before mine dropped the ball on parenting. It was enough for many of us to say, "I don't want to raise my children the way I was raised." So I rewarded my children for every little and big thing—a good grade, a nice word, helping out in the neighborhood. And you know what? Everything is good that way. It's always better to do it through love.

— Bernie Mac

Billy Bob Thornton

Daddy Dossier

Screen star Billy Bob Thornton grew up in Hot Springs, Arkansas, where his father was a teacher and a coach. Billy Bob began his career as a musician playing the drums in a band called Tres Hombres.

In 1981, he decided to become an actor and screenwriter. He wrote and starred in *One False Move* and then wrote, directed, and starred in the critically acclaimed *Sling Blade.* He's also had roles in *The Man Who Wasn't There, Bad Santa, Bad News Bears, The Alamo,* and *School for Scoundrels.*

He has four children: Amanda, William, Harry, and Bella.

What I Know about . . . Being the Fun Dad

Well, my kids do love coming over. They call my place the rock-and-roll home! I have a real recording studio, and musicians like Warren Zevon and Jewel have come over to play. I think it's great to have fun while teaching the kids about something as important as music. My kids are allowed to play. They know about cutting a record, and they love it.

The point is to give your children a creative outlet. You don't need a recording studio in your basement. Just get a few old instruments at a garage sale and jam.

What I Know about . . . Little League Parents

Now every kid gets a trophy, which I think makes children lazy. It wasn't like that when I was a kid. Athletic competition was fierce when I was growing up . . . yet I don't believe in these crazy, insane Marine-sergeant coaches. But I also don't believe things should be handed to kids. There's too much obsession with being the best or being a loser or misfit. Just go out there and try. Don't feel bad about yourself if you're trying—that's what I tell my kids.

Sports are supposed to serve as an example of life for kids, and life doesn't hand you trophies for doing nothing. I played Little League, and I'll never forget the first game where I pitched. I struck out ten batters, and it was the best day of my life. I had a curveball a little early—you're not supposed to have one at age 12, but I did. It's one of my fondest life memories.

What I Know about . . . Being Strict

I'm the least strict dad in the world. But my boys' mother is a very good disciplinarian. Basically, I let them do whatever they want within reason. They even came to the set of *Bad Santa.* I made them wear earphones so they couldn't hear the dialogue.

When we were growing up, we weren't exposed to as much as kids are now. You can't show them much. You have to be careful.

What changes when you become a mother? What <u>doesn't</u> change? Your view of the world changes. I don't see anything the same anymore. My first reaction was: "How do we have war when all of us in this world are mothers and fathers?" After having my children, I just can't wrap my head around war anymore.

— Téa Leoni

Carnie Wilson

Mommy Material

Born the daughter of Beach Boy legend Brian Wilson, Carnie Wilson has overcome a lifelong struggle with obesity to achieve personal satisfaction, professional success, and new dimensions of physical and emotional health. As a young child growing up in the fast lane, Carnie turned to food for comfort. As she grew into adulthood and achieved success with the multiplatinum pop group Wilson Phillips, her dysfunctional relationship with food led to life-threatening morbid obesity.

In the summer of 1999, she made the dramatic decision to undergo state-of-the-art weight-loss surgery live over the Internet. Over the next two years, her life was transformed as she lost more than 150 pounds, married the man of her dreams, and fashioned a new future of exciting career opportunities. Now dedicated to helping others, Carnie speaks to groups about weight loss and other health issues. She has continued her recording and television career and is also the author of three books including *I'm Still Hungry* and *To Serve with Love.*

She and her husband, Rob Bonfiglio, are the proud parents of an adorable toddler, Lola.

What I Know about . . .
Worrying During the Early Days of Pregnancy

I was really nervous about being pregnant for many reasons. I worried that I was going to be really hormonal and cry every day. I also worried about myself physically because I've had several abdominal surgeries, including gastric bypass, and I've had a hernia corrected. So I was physically apprehensive, as many women are when they find out they're pregnant.

What helped me not worry was finding a hobby. I started knitting. It's a really good pastime because it takes your mind off of everything else.

Make sure that you take time to rest when you're pregnant. If you're like me, then you're very active and almost never sit down. I was always on my feet running around. What helped me in the beginning of my pregnancy was my hobby, because I had to sit to make blankets, sweaters, and hats. It feels really good in those early days to do something for the baby.

I also spent some of my relaxing time sitting in front of the computer talking to other pregnant women. The Internet is a great resource. Of course it's better to talk with friends and family who've had children, but it's also nice to reach out to others. One word of caution during the early days of your pregnancy: Don't get too freaked out about all the stuff you read on the Internet. There are horror stories out there that are very upsetting. Just remember that every pregnancy is different.

What I Know about . . .
Making Love During Pregnancy

During the early days of my pregnancy, I wondered if making love would hurt the baby. The answer is no. Every single doctor will tell you that—but, of course, check with *your* doctor, because every pregnancy is different.

Actually, this was just one of my many questions in those days. I'd also wonder, *Why is the baby not moving yet?* I called my sister, Wendy, ten times a day. Don't worry if you need to make those phone calls to friends and family. Every question on your mind is important, and every pregnant woman has been there at one point in her life.

I remember thinking, *Oh my God, there's this rush of heat going through my ankles. Is that a sign that a miscarriage is coming on? Is it normal to feel this sensation?* I called my doctor over that one, and she didn't mind. Your physician is there to ease your mind. It doesn't hurt to make those calls, because it's good to ask as many questions as possible. My doctor was really cool, and she always answered my questions, including: "Is it normal for a lot of freckles to come out on your face and under your eyes during pregnancy? Is it normal for your nipples to turn darker during pregnancy? Is it normal to feel a pulling sensation down below?" (By the way, the answer was yes to all of the above.)

What I Know about . . .
Emergencies During Pregnancy

I was bleeding in week seven of my pregnancy. That was super-scary. My advice is to immediately call your doctor, but don't panic. My bleeding was just a clot that needed to come out. I had to rest a couple of days and then I was fine.

I also found out that my hands and feet were hurting. In fact, that pain would wake me up in the morning. My hands ached, and eventually I could barely make a fist. My doctor assured me that this was fine.

I was also a bit concerned about my dreams. I wondered, *Is it normal during pregnancy to dream that your dog took acid?* My dreams were that weird. One night I had one where I was going up and down elevators all day long. It's quite normal to have strange dreams when you're pregnant.

What I Know about . . .
Choosing Your Advisors

Every time I asked my mother for some parenting advice, she'd say to me, "That was a long time ago and I don't remember." I think it's better to ask your sister—if you have one—for specific pregnancy tips. Don't get upset with your mother. Remember that she gave birth to you many years ago. She'll remember little things and tell you funny stories, but your sister is closer to having children in many cases.

By the way, my mom was so funny during my pregnancy. She'd say to me, "Carnie, don't push on your belly." I still did it, and I'd say, "Go, Lola!" That would freak my mom out!

What I Know about . . .
Husbands and Pregnancy

I think many husbands are a bit freaked out during the first month of pregnancy. In fact, both Rob and I were really scared at first. He stayed a bit clear of everything because he was nervous. Then all of a sudden that passed and he was really into it. So, give your husband a bit of a break and let him come to you.

Rob is a musician, and he was into playing music for the baby when she was developing her hearing. We both agreed that the baby could feel vibrations, so we wanted to play her beautiful melodies. We even bought a special baby music kit where you could hook it up to an iPod and play her songs. We'd turn on the music and put the earpieces around my stomach . . . Lola went crazy.

Rob also began to really talk to her when she was in my belly. He'd put his mouth right up to my stomach and say, "Hi, Lola. It's Daddy. I love you. What are you doing in there? Are you playing? I can't wait to meet you. It's Daddy saying good-bye for now. I love you."

Tears would be rolling down my face. It was the most pure, bonding, beautiful, loving thing you could ever imagine and feel. She wasn't even born yet, but her father was showing so much sensitivity. I could feel that special love inside his chest. It was intense and wonderful.

I'll never forget the night Rob took out his guitar and we sang Beatles songs. Lola went bonkers in my belly. She was kicking me everywhere. We kept singing, "Here Comes the Sun" and then launched into a George Harrison song called "My Sweet Lord." We went totally nuts, but our baby went even crazier.

One particular womb favorite for Lola was Frank Sinatra. We'd play him, and whenever the orchestra or strings or horns would come in, I swear to God, she'd dance. And at one point I said to Rob, "I don't know whether we're scaring her or she loves it." I think she loved it, because when she hears strings and horns now, she looks up and sways back and forth. It's so cute.

Every single day after that, I began saying her name, and she always responded by kicking me wildly.

What I Know about . . . Miracles

You really don't know what pregnancy will be like until you go through it. What surprised me the most is that those nine months go by fast. What's so lovely is that the love keeps growing and growing, too. Your baby starts out as an idea and a wish. At least that's how it worked for us. We planned our baby. She's our first child, and we were so lucky that we got pregnant right away. We'll always know that she was made out of pure love, and that she was a wish who became a reality.

I guess that reality didn't really sink in until I felt her kick for the first time. This was at 16 weeks. I ate three pieces of See's chocolate and was resting on my side looking at a Sharper Image catalog. All of a sudden, I felt this tiny flutter in the center of my belly. It was like someone was tapping on a drum from the inside—she went, "Boom, boom, boom." My heart started pounding, and I got really nervous. Then I smiled and thought, *Oh my God. Is that the baby? It's alive in there!* Then I actually thought, *Is that the baby, or is it gas?*

After that moment, I started to really pay attention to my belly. The flutter got bigger and bigger. Suddenly, she was really kicking and moving. It felt like a little alien was in there, but I hate when people say that word. It's a little *person* in there.

I loved lying in bed in the later months and watching my stomach move from side to side. She would kick so hard that my body would jerk to the right. As the baby grew, the kicking actually slowed down because there wasn't much room for her to kick. That's when I felt her pushing, stretching, and squirming. I felt her knees and elbows. I'd wonder, *Is she really bored in there?*

I also noticed her sleeping patterns. When I was hungry, she'd kick me. Then I'd eat, and she'd become hyper for a few minutes and then go to sleep. If only she would have stopped kicking my cervix and bladder. *Ouch!*

What I Know about . . .
Surviving the Early Days of Motherhood

Sleep when the baby is sleeping. But if you have too many things to get done, it's really hard. That's the time you do the dishes, that's the time you take a shower, that's the time you make your phone calls. It's so difficult—and that's why managing your time is so important. And drink lots of water.

And of course, enjoy every moment that you have with your baby.

Children are a lot like pancakes: You sort of get messy with the first one, and you get better at it the second time around!

— **Kelly Ripa,** talk-show hostess with the mostess on *Live with Regis and Kelly*

Joan Rivers

Granny Gossip

Can she talk? The answer is yes! Brooklyn native Joan Rivers graduated from Barnard College, where she studied anthropology before going on to become one of America's premier stand-up comedians.

She got her break guest-hosting for Johnny Carson, which led to her own talk show. Most recently, she has hosted red-carpet events for E! Entertainment Television and now does pre-awards-show coverage for the TV Guide Channel. She's also developing a male version of *The View* as a daytime talk show.

Joan is mom to TV broadcaster Melissa Rivers and grandmother to Edgar Cooper Endicott, 6—named after Joan's late husband, Edgar.

What I Know about . . . Being a Grandmother

One of the great parts of being a grandmother is the stealing. They'll never book a five-year-old for taking a Hermès pocketbook . . . just kidding.

Honestly, being a grandmother is the most wonderful thing in the world. I do things with my grandson that I never did with Melissa. We go bowling! We have bowling shirts that say RED CARPET ROLLERS! It's this stupid shirt, but I love it. My grandson, his friends, Melissa, and I meet at the local bowling alley. It's hilarious that I'll do anything with him because I adore him.

I think it's important that you also make the time. I take a week off every summer and another off in the winter to spend time with my grandson and Melissa. Don't tell me that the queen of England wants me to come over for dinner, because I'm not available. We go away, have wonderful dinners, and just experience great times.

I want my grandson to remember Grandma spoiled him. Everything I didn't do with Melissa as her mother comes out with him. I've actually said to him, "Come on! We don't need vegetables. Let's go eat two ice creams for dinner." Melissa's eyes will roll into the back of her head, but she allows me—I'm the grandmother.

What I Know about . . .
Cultivating a Child's Sense of Humor

My grandson has a great sense of humor. I knew it when he was in the high chair, and I said to Melissa, "He's funny and he gets us." I've told Melissa that he'll be Larry David or Neil Simon someday. The key is to just let him tell his jokes and laugh. I don't think a child can be too silly. Let him explore his funny side, although I think humor is in the DNA. My father was funny. My sister the lawyer is funny, and she even makes juries laugh. My grandson has gotten the DNA, thank God. I tell him, "If you can laugh, you can go through anything in life." It's good advice for everyone.

Time-Out

The whole point of being in a relationship and having children is that you learn to love unconditionally. . . . While my creative energy is incredibly important to me, being a parent and having friends and a relationship is even more important. I'm into nurturing these days. Quite simply, motherhood has changed my life. For one thing, now I have to be so much more organized with my time. I don't really have free time anymore. . . .

It's so funny that my children are so talented. Lourdes does me! Lola also likes Mary J. Blige and the Spice Girls. I'm like, "Don't do my act. Do more of them, honey!"

— Madonna

Adam Beach

Daddy Dossier

Adam Beach is a Saulteaux Indian who hails from Manitoba, Canada. He lost both parents in separate accidents when he was only eight.

Adam pursued his dream of acting, beginning his career on TV's *Spirit Rider* and *Lonesome Dove: The Series.* He's starred in movies including *Smoke Signals; Mystery, Alaska; Windtalkers;* and *Now & Forever.* Most recently, he played World War II Marine Ira Hayes in Clint Eastwood's epic film *Flags of Our Fathers.*

Adam is a member of the Ojibwa nation and speaks frequently on behalf of the group First Nation Youth. He has two sons, Noah, 10; and Luke, 8.

What I Know about . . . Doing as I Do

I just try to make sure my nature speaks to who and what I am. I want my two children to look up to me as a role model and say, "I love my dad because he's the best man." My kids are eight and ten. My best parental advice is that your kids are looking everywhere and anywhere for direction and role models. How your children will lead their future lives starts in your household—it's important, and your responsibility as a parent is to be an example of what life should be out there.

If your child sidesteps and becomes involved in something negative, it stems from the household. There's something not being told. By this I mean that a lot of people live in denial. They don't want to admit the mistakes in their homes.

The bottom line is, I'm not strict at all. I just represent myself to my kids in the best possible way. I don't smoke cigarettes. I don't drink. I don't do drugs. I'm passive, but I do stand up when I need to stand up. I don't want weak children.

I'm a role model for Native American children, too. There aren't many Native Americans who have this type of success. I tell my children that we must use our success to drive our nations of people to pick themselves up. I want to give them hope that they can achieve anything. I go to conferences and give speeches to kids. I do a lot of this to show my own children that you must give back.

I hope the sacrifices I make for my kids will lead them to act by the example I set for them when they were younger. And someday I hope they'll remember the way their father was. I'm their first role model.

Time-out

I know a little bit more but not much.
My advice is to just relax. And get a good nanny.

— **Brian Cox,** the star of *Running with Scissors* and
X2: X-Men United, who became a father
again in his late 50s

Dr. Erika Schwartz

Mommy Material

Dr. Erika is a nationally recognized patients' advocate who's spent 33 years practicing medicine. She has authored four books: *Natural Energy* (Berkley Trade, 1999); *The Hormone Solution* (Warner Books, 2002); *The 30-Day Natural Hormone Plan* (Warner Books, 2004); and *The Teen Weight-Loss Solution* (HarperCollins, 2004).

Dr. Erika also lectures on health and wellness issues to corporations and writes a weekly magazine column read by ten million people. In addition, she's hosted her own TV show and a PBS pledge special and has appeared on CBS's *The Early Show,* ABC's *The View,* Fox News Channel's *The Chris Matthews Show,* and many more programs. She's written and been the subject of articles for many publications, including *The Wall Street Journal, W, Glamour, Women's Health, USA Today, The New York Times,* the *Boston Herald, Vogue, Shape, Self,* and *Natural Health.*

Dr. Erika has a remarkable backstory. Born in Communist Romania, her family escaped to Italy when she was 15. She later moved with her parents to the U.S., where she obtained her undergraduate degree at NYU on a full academic scholarship. She received her M.D. cum laude from SUNY Downstate's College of Medicine. At age 28, she became the first woman and the youngest physician to run the trauma center at Westchester Medical Center. In private practice she's cared for more than 100,000 patients.

Her kids are 21 and 29, and she's also raised several stepchildren.

What I Know about . . . Wise Discipline

I think that parents don't know the difference between disciplining a child and listening to him or her. I believe that's a very big thing in parenting. Many moms and dads refuse to set limits when their children are young. This is the worst type of parenting because actually you're abdicating your parental role, and everything will just get worse as your child becomes a teen. I think these parents are very afraid to confront their kids and take responsibility for creating a positive outcome. Please remember that good parenting is all about taking responsibility.

There are a few rules to remember with your child. You have to be respectful, kind, and honest with the kid you're disciplining. If you think about it . . . well, those are also the basic rules of life.

What I Know about . . . Saying No

I think most parents get carried away with saying, "No, no, no, no, no!" to their young children. This doesn't give kids much room to become people who truly learn why they've been told no. What happens if you just say "No, no, no, no, no" without explanations is that you wind up with a kid who's constantly bucking the system. It's just normal to fight about a senseless no.

I think you should pick your battles wisely with a young child. For instance, let's say your little boy who's five wants to wear green and red together in the middle of the summer. It's okay and not that important. You don't want to battle that one, because with small children it's important to choose your discussions based on importance. In fact, there shouldn't be "battles" at all. I look upon conflict as if it's an educational opportunity.

Let's say that your child wakes up on Saturday morning and is whining that she wants to go to a water park because it's hot out, but you can't do it on that day. You can say, "I'd love to take you to that water park, but we can't go today. We'll have to go another time." That isn't a fight, but a statement.

You have to be an adult to be a parent, and most people are not adults, period. They're overgrown children. Being a grown-up means being honest with yourself and others.

What I Know about . . .
Mothers Who Do Everything and Fathers Who Do Nothing with the Kids

Maybe that father shouldn't be there. Think about it: You have a completely uninvolved father . . . what kind of message does that give your children? The husband and wife must be a team, and they need to show the children an honest, kind, and loving relationship with each other and then with the kids. This is actually teaching them how to have a great relationship.

If you have a father who doesn't participate in parenting, I wouldn't accept the situation. I'd sit him down and say, "You were a part of creating these children. I didn't have them alone, and I need you to participate in parenting them."

Many times this situation persists because of the mother. A woman with bad self-esteem and low self-confidence feels she's not worthy of support in the parenting relationship with her partner. Once she works on her own self-esteem, she'll realize that she needs to turn the rest of her life around. If her man is a workaholic, she needs to say to him, "It's not about the money we leave behind in this world. It's about the children we give to this planet and the time we enjoy while we're here."

Ultimately, if your partner will not work with you, then you should reevaluate the relationship.

What I Know about . . .
Staying Together "for the Sake of the Kids"

A lot of women will say to me, "I know the relationship is bad, and I haven't been happy for years, but we're staying together for the kids." I say that's total baloney . . . I've been divorced, and I know that the children definitely are aware when the relationship is bad, and they don't thrive. If the parents stay in a bad relationship, then no one thrives, and the children don't do well in adult relationships. Kids can see that you're in a make-believe marriage. You're much better to come from a place where honesty rules. And by the way, you can't sweep a bad marriage under the rug. Maybe that worked in the 1800s, but it doesn't work now. Everyone knows what's going on, because the children are so much more aware and so much more evolved.

I see mothers and daughters together, and it always shocks the mom when the daughter will simply say, "My parents don't have a real relationship, and I never want that in my life." The mother will say, "Well, we stay together for you and your brother." It's terrible for the child. Even worse is when the mother in a troubled relationship with her partner takes her teen daughter or son in as her buddy and confidant about the strife. You're not allowing your child to be a real teenager in that case. You need to allow your kids to grow up and be their own teenager and then adult. Don't force them to be your counselor just because they're in the house.

You're forcing them to be a part of your failed relationship, and it's really not right. This is their time to be carefree and grow up on their own terms.

What I Know about . . . Problem Children

I have yet to see a problem kid who wasn't created by the parent. Children only act out when they're not heard. They misbehave when they're not validated and don't feel love.

As a parent, it's like everything in life—you should vow: "I'll make it work honorably and honestly." Most parents abdicate their role and say, "The kid is bad." The kid is only as bad as you made them be.

What I Know about . . . Teen Spirit

By the time your kid becomes a teenager, you're tired. Most of us are in our 40s or older when our children become teens. At that age, our careers, relationships, and social lives become very important; and we're a bit weary at times of parenting because we've been doing it most of our lives. We don't want to deal with any more problems, and if there are problems, we want them to go away.

Parents are tired. They lose interest. The worst of it is that people aren't brave, and they don't want to confront anything. The hard thing is that you have to face many issues with teenagers. Remember that I say that kids act out when they don't feel validated or loved. If you ignore a teenager, he or she will act out even more.

One of my patients came in and said, "I can't stand my kid. She's ten and she's almost a teenager. She already runs the show. She yells and is so mean to me. I work so hard, and I can't deal with it." I told her, "You better deal with it. You have ten more years to deal with it, or it will become even more of a nightmare. What can you do? Ditch her?"

The mother looked at me and asked, "Well, what do I do?" I replied, "You sit down and talk to her. If your daughter says something unkind, you say to her, 'This is not acceptable.' She's ten, and she should understand those words. If the child persists in being rude, you repeat, 'If you can't speak nicely, then go to your room. Come out when you're ready to be a kind person.'"

I'll tell you another story about how the apple never falls far from the tree. I have a friend who's a psychiatrist and a great mentor. At the time of this story, my daughter was 15 and I sent her to summer school at this boarding school in Rhode Island. She wasn't getting straight A's and I wanted her to do better in school. (We're all crazy when it comes to something—and I wouldn't do the same thing today.) My daughter didn't want to go to the boarding school, yet when we went there to visit, basically I said, "You'll have to go there for the summer.

You only got B-pluses in school. You have to do better." I didn't hear her or listen to her.

Two weeks later, I got a call from the headmaster at boarding school, who said, "Your daughter has been expelled." I asked, 'Why has she been expelled?' The headmaster told me, "She had alcohol in her dorm and had a party." I was told that there were 20 kids at the party, and that my daughter had one of those little bottles of liquor that you get on an airplane. That was the only alcohol at the party. The headmaster told me, "It's illegal for kids to drink. There will be no discussion. You have to pick her up."

I called my daughter to talk to her, and she said, "I'm sorry, Mom." Then I called my friend the psychiatrist, and I asked, "What am I doing wrong?" She said, "The apple doesn't fall far from the tree. And you have to listen to a very important message in your life that you give others, which is about being brave and honorable. Your daughter was actually being brave in taking a stand against boarding school, but she just didn't have the skills that you have. Since you didn't hear her, what she did was perform an act to get your attention. She didn't have the skills to be brave in any other way."

It was the most important moment of my life as a parent. The moral of the story is: If you don't listen, your child won't do well.

(By the way, my daughter who was involved in this incident is now an attorney.)

What I Know about . . .
Not Competing with Your Teenage Daughter

When my younger daughter was about 11 and she started sprouting breasts, it was a very sweet time in our lives—the cutest thing ever. My daughter, her girl-friend, the child's mom, and I went shopping at Urban Outfitters. The mother of this girl was going through a breakup. She was a very sexy woman who had a very sexy body. At the time, we were in our early 40s, and the other mom started trying on very provocative clothes. I whispered to her, "I think this is your daughter's time."

What I'm saying here is that as mothers, we need to let our daughters become comfortable with being sexy. If the mother competes, it's going to be a problem. In this case, my daughter's friend developed an eating disorder, although I'm glad to report that she's healed and is fine now. If the mother is trying to be ultrasexy, then the daughter can't compete. It creates serious problems in many families. There's so much plastic surgery now, and women are trying to stay young forever. They forget that perhaps it's their daughters' time to be sexy and to be noticed by guys.

What I Know about . . . Divorce

One final thought on this topic: Many mothers are bitter because they're going through a divorce. The husband has walked out, and what they do is spill their venom onto the daughter who's at home with them. These women complain and complain about the man who left them. The message the daughter receives is that all men are bad and they'll never have a good relationship. The mother is practically yelling, "Look what your father did to me! He did a horrible thing, and now you can't trust men." The girl goes out there with a jaded view, and she's full of mistrust.

Mothers should be telling their daughters that relationships can be great and extremely fulfilling. I'm married and very happy because I'm in a great relationship. I tell my kids that you can have a great relationship if you're an adult who's kind and honest and you take responsibility for creating a positive outcome.

*It's like a whole new dimension in emotion
that I've never experienced. It's crazy.*

— **Gwyneth Paltrow** on loving her children,
Apple and Moses

René Syler

Mommy Material

René Syler has been an anchor of CBS News' *The Early Show* since October 2002, when it debuted in its current four-anchor format. She has conducted one-on-one interviews with First Lady Laura Bush, Colin Powell, and Senator John McCain; as well as NASA's first female shuttle commander, Eileen Collins. She anchored from Punta Gorda, Florida, reporting on the aftermath of Hurricane Charley; and from Washington, D.C., covering the events and ceremonies of President Ronald Reagan's funeral.

Born at Scott Air Force Base in Illinois, René grew up in Sacramento, California, and graduated from California State University, Sacramento, in 1987 with a degree in psychology. She's an active member of the National Association of Black Journalists and was a recipient of the 2004 Gracie Allen Award for Individual Achievement for Best Anchor in honor of her breast-cancer series. (Even before her own breast-cancer scare, she was very active in numerous causes related to this issue.) American Women in Radio and Television also named her Television Personality of the Year in 1997.

René is married to Buff Parham, with whom she has two children, Casey, 10; and Cole, 8.

What I Know about . . .
Being the Best Mother

I guess my advice is very out there and esoteric. I remember that I was pregnant with Casey, and I was all atwitter. I couldn't believe that I was bringing another life into this world. Would I be well equipped for the job? An older woman sensed my anxiety and saw me eating nervously one day. She walked over and said to me, "You know, nobody can be as good a mother to that baby as you can be."

Can I just tell you that those words stuck with me through all the things I've done as a parent. I've remembered them every time I wanted to second-guess myself. When I feel like I'm doing an inadequate job, I remember that woman saying that no one can be a better mother to Casey or Cole. I hear her words.

The point is that you have to trust your gut. So much of parenting is flying blind and going on instinct. You can read dozens of manuals about what to expect when you're expecting. All of that stuff flies out of your head when your child is born. It's like, "Now what?" You're looking at your baby, and he or she looks at you. And somehow you make it through by trusting yourself.

What I Know about . . . Guilt and Saying Sorry

It's so hard for women, because we feel like we have to be perfect all the time. We have to be the perfect mate, the perfect worker, and the perfect mother. I like to think that you need to be good enough. Yet, I still struggle with being perfect every single day. Then I'll stop and convince myself that I'm striving. I can't beat myself up when I'm not perfect if I'm striving.

One day I was driving my kids around town. I was so excited because I picked them up from school, and I had the whole afternoon planned. Then my cell phone rang. It was one of my daughter's friends, who said, "You were supposed to meet us." I completely spaced out on a playdate. I turned to my daughter, and in a heartfelt voice, said, "Mommy screwed up." She said, "That's okay, Mommy. You have a lot on your plate!"

I've learned that it's okay to admit your shortcomings to your kids. Then they'll learn an important lesson, which is that no one is perfect.

What I Know about . . . Feeling like a Good Mom

Sometimes I'm so wildly successful as a mother that I start to feel very good about myself. An hour later, I'm a miserable failure. You can have these highs and lows in the same hour.

I leave at 4 in the morning every single day for my job. I struggle with: "Am I doing enough?" Halloween is coming up, and it's the worst for me. What can I dress these kids in this year? Will it be fun for them? I'm still trying to come up with something. Why didn't I volunteer enough at school? My daughter said, "Can you be in the class, Mom?" I told her, "That's a full-time job, honey." My daughter was very understanding, while I put pressure on myself. You simply have to give yourself a break and realize that you can't have every moment be the best one. You can only try to make the best out of every moment.

What I Know about . . . the Dinner Table

One of our biggest challenges is the dinner table. My family only gets to eat one major meal a week together because of my husband's commute to his job. We only have this one dinner, so I used to place so much pressure on it to be this Norman Rockwell setting. I had dreams of the homemade lasagna with creamed corn and fresh spinach. I had dreams that my kids would actually eat the spinach and no one would complain that this is actually a vegetable.

Fast-forward to reality. In real life, I do make these major family dinners, but the kids are complaining the entire time. They don't want the homemade lasagna. All they want is chicken nuggets and waffle fries. All of a sudden, they're not in their seats—they're up, down, and all around. It was time to stop putting so much pressure on this one meal.

I still make the nice dinner, but all I care about is if enough food goes in their gullet. After they eat, I don't make the kids sit at the table to the point where they can't stand it anymore. I dismiss them so my husband and I can have time together. You have to cultivate the primary relationship, too—and you can do that nicely over homemade lasagna and creamed corn.

*I did a lot of walking during the pregnancy; and
I had a wonderful, much-longed-for natural delivery.
I was in labor 24 hours, and he came out completely
beautifully. It was a triumphant birth, and it laid
a lot of ghosts to rest for me. It was incredible to
experience being able to do it totally naturally.*

— Kate Winslet

Abby Ellin

Abby Ellin is the author of *Teenage Waistland: A Former Fat Kid Weighs In on Living Large, Losing Weight, and How Parents Can (and Can't) Help.* Her Website is **www.teenagewaistland.com**.

Abby also writes for *The New York Times*'s Style section. She spent six years at fat camp: two as a camper and four as a counselor. About her work with overweight kids, she says, "I can relate to them. I feel for them."

What I Know about . . .
Childhood Obesity

Childhood obesity is occurring at an epidemic rate in America. It really hits me hard because I had a weight problem as a child. I'll never forget when my grandmother said, "You can't come visit me in Florida unless you lose ten pounds." Well, I didn't lose those ten pounds. Even as a child, I knew that you don't lose weight until you're ready.

We know about addiction now, and that the person who's addicted doesn't work on getting better until they're ready. You don't stop the behavior until you can say: "I'm done. I'm tired of being fat, drunk, or whatever." To be able to say those words as a child is quite ludicrous.

I was 12 when my grandmother told me that I couldn't visit her in Florida. It really did hurt my feelings.

I interviewed a lot of children in my book as well as parents of overweight kids. The kids who were obese told me that all they really wanted was unconditional love. They said that they didn't want to feel as if they had to look a certain way or behave in a certain way for their parents to love them.

The first thing to do when you see your child overeating and gaining weight is not to wait and let the problem escalate. Go to a doctor and see if there's a medical issue. If there isn't a medical issue, then it might be an emotional one. Tell your child, "I'm here for you. If you want my help and support, I'll give it to you, but I'm not going to bug you about food and exercise. I'm not going to harass you." That's truly the way to approach a child who's gaining weight.

You should also reinforce that your house is a healthy and positive environment. To do this, you must exhibit the behavior you want your kids to display. If you sit on the couch all night with a giant spoon in a gallon of ice cream, it's hard not to expect your child to follow suit. If you drag out the bag of chips and call it dinner, then your child will think this is fine and the norm. But if you eat salads and healthy proteins along with fruits and vegetables, then *that* becomes the norm.

Practice what you've told your child. You let them know that you wouldn't bug them, and you shouldn't pester them each time you see them eating something high in calories. Don't say, "Put down that ice cream and cake. What are you doing to your body? Don't you know you're gaining weight?" This is the worst type of parenting, because each and every time, the child will simply eat more. This becomes a terrible cycle of you policing food and your child rebelling by eating more.

The biggest key is to stock the house with healthy foods—lean protein, fruits, and veggies. It's tough if you have other kids in the house who aren't fat. As a parent, you might begin to think, *Why is Timmy being denied? He doesn't have a weight problem. He could eat a few cookies.* The answer to that one is that a member of the family is obese, and to help him or her, it takes an entire-family effort. When someone in your family has a serious health problem, then everybody should band together, even if they can't have a bag of Oreos that night.

The bottom line on children and food does fall back on the parent. Kids want structure. They need it and crave it, especially ones who are dealing with weight issues. They truly want the boundaries, and they also want their parents to *be* parents and set limits. Children who overeat are often testing the limits. The responsibility of the parent is to keep tabs and rein the child back in. If you give in every single day and drive to McDonald's to get the McNuggets before dinner, then you're not setting limits.

It makes me sad that you see so many obese children these days. People are talking about this phenomenon, and they say, "Oh, it's just all that fast food out there." I don't agree that this is the reason for childhood obesity. The reality is, the parenting isn't there to guide a child to proper food choices. If you're poor, it's harder to avoid the temptations of a quick, cheap meal of fast food, but you have to think of your kid's health. You have to be the parent and tell your children that their body needs to be healthy.

Obese kids are actually crying out for their parents to care about their health. Listen to them, and help them find the love that they're really craving.

*My daughter has a problem picking
things up in her room. So if you leave your
clothes on the floor, we put them in a bin
bag. She has to earn them back by being tidy.*

— **Madonna**

*When I had my second son, my love wasn't
mixed up with searching for something else.
I found a home. It really profoundly changed me.
I was one of those kids who wanted to be a mother
from the time I was about five. I'd go to the playground
and ask the moms if I could look after their kids. I guess
I was looking for something. And having the children
has made me more passionate. About everything.*

— **Jennifer Connelly**

Diane Lane

Mommy Material

New York native Diane Lane began acting as a child, which was only natural, since her parents are acting coach Burt Lane and nightclub singer Colleen Farrington. By age 6, Diane was onstage, and at 13 she was cast in George Roy Hill's film *A Little Romance* with Sir Laurence Olivier. She landed on the cover of *Time* magazine for her performance.

As a teenager, she starred in classic films such as *Rumble Fish, The Outsiders,* and *Streets of Fire.* Her other films credits include *The Cotton Club, Chaplin, A Walk on the Moon, Unfaithful,* and *Under the Tuscan Sun.*

Diane has a daughter named Eleanor, 13, with her first husband, actor Christopher Lambert. She's currently married to actor Josh Brolin.

What I Know about . . .
Motherhood at an Early Age

Motherhood gave me a much more important priority. I didn't care what Hollywood thought of me, but rather what my daughter thought of me. I was a same-sex role model for a child. I had a high level of accountability.

It's difficult to be the bad guy and say no in your house. That's harder than saying no to a role. I had to grow a spine . . . and I didn't know I didn't have a spine until I had a child and had to grow one. I kept thinking, *What if she doesn't like me? Will she run away?*

What I Know about . . .
Remarrying and Combining Families

I can't even calculate how my life has changed since marrying Josh . . . the changes are so immense. I went from being a single parent who was living in a bubble to a woman whose house is now full of people. It's a shared life, and it's not even "my" house anymore. They all have rooms, and I don't. I say, "I'll just be in the kitchen." But I love my new life and appreciate it. It's not quiet ever—and I love it that way.

Time-out

If you have a fussy eater, you can take omega-3 fish oil for added nutrients that are so good for brain development. You throw it right in their food, and they never taste it. You can also put pureed spinach in their food, which has brain-boosting vitamins.

— **Kelly Ripa** on dealing with tough kiddie-food issues

Mark Wahlberg

Daddy Dossier

Boston native Mark Wahlberg grew up in Dorchester, the working-class section of Beantown, with five brothers and three sisters. A former rapper turned underwear model for Calvin Klein, Marky Mark (his music stage name) has become respected actor Mark Wahlberg. He's starred in *Renaissance Man; The Basketball Diaries; Boogie Nights; The Italian Job;* and most recently, *Invincible* and the mobster film *The Departed.*

Mark and girlfriend Rhea Durham are the parents of Ella Rae, 3; and Michael, 1.

What I Know about . . .
My Baby Has a Fever!

Presents certainly do help. My daughter had a cold the other day, so I took her to the FAO Schwarz toy store to make her feel better. I know you're not supposed to do that all the time, but I felt so bad when I heard her coughing. I would have bought her whatever she wanted. She only wanted a little Hello Kitty and a Get Well Elmo, which was about the cutest thing in the entire world.

Today I tucked her in with her Get Well Elmo so they could both be sick together. I think just the tucking in and talking to her made her feel better. But Elmo didn't hurt. He had a little cast and a Band-Aid on his leg. I know I'm perceived as a tough guy, but truly this was just too adorable. It even made *me* feel better!

He rushed into the room, and he saw
some other woman's feet in the stirrups.

— **Maggie Gyllenhaal** on how her significant other,
Peter Sarsgaard, accidentally walked in on another
woman in the gynecologist's office during an appoint-
ment (by the way, he was in the right room when
baby daughter Ramona was born last year)

Reese Witherspoon

Mommy Material

A-list actress Reese Witherspoon hails from New Orleans, where her father was a military surgeon and her mother was a nurse. She grew up for several years in Wiesbaden, Germany, where her father was working, and then the family moved to Nashville.

She began her career as a child actress with roles in *The Man in the Moon, Jack the Bear,* and *A Far Off Place.* She's subsequently starred in such movies as *Pleasantville, Election, Cruel Intentions, Legally Blonde,* and *Sweet Home Alabama.* She won a Best Actress Oscar for playing mom, wife, and singer June Carter Cash in the hit film *Walk the Line.*

Reese has two children, Ava, 7; and Deacon, 3.

What I Know about . . . Balancing It All

How do I balance it all? Very carefully. I just try to take care of the kids first and sort out their lives and their schools before I worry about myself. If the kids are happy, then the parents are happy. Once I have all that sorted out, it's easier to get on with my life.

For instance, my daughter is starting kindergarten this year. I took a little time off to be there for her on her first few days. I was sure she'd be fine, but I knew that *I* wouldn't be fine! I knew I'd be crying and she'd be like, "Mommy, I'm having fun. You can get out of here now!"

What I Know about . . . Being a Role Model

I think as soon as I became a mother, I felt a responsibility for being a role model. That's the nature of being a mom. You think, *Oh no, this person will look up to me.* I take it very seriously, and it's a big responsibility. All parents should feel the same way.

What I Know about . . . Forgetting about Work When You're a Mom

Children are very good at keeping you grounded. They'll throw up on your shoes before an awards ceremony. That's when you remember, "I'm a Mom first—before anything and everything!"

Time-out

I think it's good to keep the stroller as scarce as possible once your child can walk. I see all these kids, and they're so big—they can walk, and they're being pushed around all day. My daughter is very active, but it's so much better for them to move and negotiate the terrain. They also get tired faster. They're down quicker, and they want to take a nap. I believe in children getting their exercise. They're more physically able to meet the challenges. . . .

Oh, and by the way, I haven't watched E.T. with my own kids. My daughter is two. She's still too young. I know we'll watch it together someday, but I want to wait a few more years.

— **Henry Thomas,** aka Elliott in *E.T.*

Jodie Foster

Mommy Material

Jodie Foster's career began when she was three, flashing her bare bottom in a Coppertone ad. As a child actress, she had roles in *One Little Indian, Bugsy Malone, Freaky Friday,* and *Taxi Driver.* She attended Yale University, where she studied English literature and graduated magna cum laude in 1985.

As an adult, Jodie won Best Actress Oscars for *The Accused* and *The Silence of the Lambs.* She has also directed two movies, *Little Man Tate* and *Home for the Holidays;* and is the proud mom of Charles, 8; and Kit, 5.

What I Know about . . . Worrying

You want to keep your children from any kind of pain—that's the biggest worry. It's funny, but I never really cared about getting on a ride at an amusement park or being on a plane going through turbulence before I became a mother. The second you have a child, you really care about your life. You're like, "What should

I do?" You don't want your child to be left without a parent. In fact, this idea is so horrendously painful to you that it keeps you on your toes.

I think that there's a strange symbiotic, primal connection between you and your children at the same time. There's this part of your identity that's consumed with protecting them. But you can't really protect another individual from harm all the time. You really can't prevent every scraped knee. You can try, but ultimately, there's only so much you can keep them from in life. That's excruciatingly painful, but it's a fact of life.

What I Know about . . . Myself as a Mom

I learned so many things about myself after I became a mother. I thought that I was going to have to figure out how to juggle the kids and my life. What I didn't realize is that I'd be completely consumed by my children, and the rest of my life would become so little a priority. I think it's fine to feel that way.

What I Know about . . . My Own Mother

I catch myself saying the exact same things my mother would say to me. My mom used to say, "I don't really care about Johnny and what his parents do. I have no interest in what's happening in their house. It's too bad." Or she'd say, "Because I said so."

Now, I'm like, *Why do I have to do that? Why do I say "Because I said so"?* That sounds really bad, but you get to a certain point where it's like, "I don't have to give you ten explanations. It's just because I said so, and that's all there is to it!"

What I Know about . . . Independence

All of this doesn't mean that I don't have independence from my children, too, and that I don't have a creative life aside from being a mother. Having your own interests and maintaining them is very healthy. I'd be crazed if I didn't have those interests. I think that it's important to distinguish yourself from your children.

*If Aidan's crying when I'm singing, I'll try
to change the key and see what he does, which
is usually stop crying. He's a new form of entertainment around here. And if there's ever a <u>Baby Idol</u>
show, watch out. I'm about to put a guitar in his
hands—a baby guitar. You can't start too soon.*

— **Bo Bice,** *American Idol* finalist,
on his new "bandmate" and son

Kelsey Grammer

Daddy Dossier

Five-time Emmy® Award winner Kelsey Grammer played the beloved TV shrink Dr. Frasier Crane on his own series, *Frasier,* as well as the hit show *Cheers.* He also voices Sideshow Bob on the animated show *The Simpsons,* and Stinky Pete in Disney's *Toy Story 2.*

A native of the Virgin Islands, Kelsey grew up with his mother and grandmother in New Jersey and Florida. He studied at the Juilliard School and then made his mark doing classical theater on Broadway, including *Macbeth* and *Othello.* In 1984, he bellied up to the bar on the hit series *Cheers,* where his droll wit earned him a nationwide following of Frasier fans. He recently played Beast in *X-Men: The Last Stand.*

Kelsey is married to Camille Grammer and is the father of Spencer, 21 (with his first wife); Greer, 14 (with his second wife); Mason Olivia, 5 (delivered via a surrogate mother); and Jude Gordon, 2 (also delivered via a surrogate).

What I Know about . . .
Being an Older Dad

I'm a calmer guy now than when I had my first kid. I got a second chance at parenting, which has been great. I spend a lot of time with my kids because that counts so much. I have to say that the time has been as important for them as it has for me.

I love being with my five-year-old daughter, because the time is extraordinary. I'm honestly rediscovering life through her eyes, which might sound clichéd, but it's true. You appreciate everything from a beautiful bird to the way the clouds dance in the sky. Children will make you appreciate your world again, if you just give them the chance. That's the beauty of being an older parent. You have the time, and you want to spend it wisely.

What I Know about . . . Parental Rules

The demands of parenting are fairly simple if you're a traditionalist like me. I think that I owe my children clarity and organization.

As for specific suggestions for other parents, I can't stress enough that you shouldn't allow the kids to be in bed with you. They need to be their own person, and they need sleep. They also have to learn how to spend that time alone. You're really not helping them by bringing them into bed with you—plus, the entire family will get sick each time the child has a sniffle.

What I Know about . . .
Things That Go Bump in the Night

When I was a little boy, I was afraid of whatever I thought lived in my bedroom closet. I was sure something was in there, living in the darkness and just waiting to come out the minute my parents snapped off my bedroom light and closed the door.

Many children experience these fears, and here's what I'd do: I'd tell the child to do what I was told as a little boy, which is, "When the lights go out, say your prayers for the night. Now, remember that your angels are there with you, and they'll remain with you until you wake up the next morning." This truly worked for me as a scared little boy.

By the way, my daughter truly isn't afraid. I played a creature with a blue face and body in the last *X-Men* film. I was afraid that Daddy would frighten her as the blue guy, so I had her come to the set and watch me get into the makeup so it wouldn't frighten her. The first time she saw me looking that way, she said, "Daddy, I'm a little bit scared." It's fine to acknowledge your child's fears, but then it's your job to make them go away. I told her, "Honey, don't I look just like one of the Teletubbies?" The fear was gone, and suddenly I was an extra-cool dad because I looked like a giant Teletubby.

*I hate ridiculous names. My weird
name has haunted me all of my life.*

— **Peaches Honeyblossom Michelle Charlotte Angel
Vanessa Geldof,** the daughter of Bob Geldof and the
late Paula Yates; author of a recent piece in *The Daily
Telegraph* on resisting giving children strange names
(by the way, her sisters are Fifi Trixibelle, Little Pixie,
and Heavenly Hiraani Tiger Lily)

Marcia Gay Harden

Mommy Material

Marcia Gay Harden was born in La Jolla, California, as the third of five children in a military family. She spent some of her youth in Greece, where she fell in love with live theater. After returning to the U.S. and graduating from the University of Texas at Austin, she earned an M.F.A. from NYU. Marcia went on to star in movies such as *Mona Lisa Smile, Casa de los Babys, Mystic River, Space Cowboys, Meet Joe Black, Flubber, The First Wives Club,* and *Pollock,* which earned her an Oscar.

Marcia and her husband, Thaddaeus Scheel, have three children—Eulala, 8; and twins Julitta and Hudson, 3.

What I Know about . . .
Listening to My Children

My eight-year-old helps me with the twins. But it's so important that I listen to her, as we're on this journey together. She's very clear and articulate, as many children are, which is why you should listen and not just dismiss what they say because they're young. My little girl will say, "Mommy, I think you love the twins better than me today." She's not acting out by saying this, but is expressing an emotion that she feels. It's not fair not to listen to her, because she's telling me what's inside of her heart. That's crucial—and I'll say, "Thank you for telling me, and now let's talk about how you're feeling."

What I Know about . . . Slowing Down

I think everyone who's a parent should edit what they're doing in life. By this I mean stop moving so fast, because you do need to slow down to deal with your children. Stop multitasking for one minute and get down on the floor with your kids—without a cell phone in the other hand. The children want your attention. They want to see you at their level and for you to join their world. So get down there with them. Focus just on them . . . even if it's only for a certain amount of time before you have to stand up and do something else. Just be sure to make them your priority without anything else going on at the same time. That's quality time.

I figured this out one day when I found myself on my cell phone while making cookies with my daughter. Isn't that ridiculous? Am I really spending time with my little girl if I'm talking to someone else and she's just sitting there stirring chocolate chips into a bowl?

The answer is: I can do better. I can stop and edit my behavior. You simply can't be that unaware of your children. It's not fair to them.

It's difficult being a mother and working at the same time. Mothering is a full-time job. Saying I'm a working mother is like saying I'm a lawyer and an anthropologist. It's hard to balance it all, but ultimately so worth it.

— **Uma Thurman**

There's no such thing as Übermom.

— **Kelly Ripa**

Nancy O'Dell

Mommy Material

Nancy O'Dell is co-anchor of *Access Hollywood,* a job she's had since 1996 when she helped launch the show. She covers the Oscars, Emmys, Grammys, Golden Globes, and American Music Awards. She also reports stories for NBC's *Today* and *Dateline NBC.* A member of the Academy of Country Music, she's hosted and served as consulting producer of USA Network's *Nashville Star,* a nationwide search for the next great country-music artist. She's also been a cohost of NBC's broadcast of the Miss USA pageant.

Hailing from South Carolina, Nancy was inducted into that state's Entertainment and Music Hall of Fame in 1998. Nancy has earned three Associated Press awards and two Society of Professional Journalists awards and is a five-time Emmy Award nominee. A summa cum laude graduate of Clemson University, she began her career at WPDE-TV in Myrtle Beach, South Carolina; and worked as morning-news anchor and crime reporter at WCBD-TV in Charleston. She was also an investigative reporter for NBC's Miami station, WTVJ.

Nancy serves as a celebrity ambassador for Childhelp, an organization dedicated to the prevention of child abuse. She's married to business executive Keith Zubchevich; is pregnant with their first child together; and is stepmother to his two children, Tyler, 10; and Carson, 6.

What I Know about . . .
Getting to Know Stepchildren

I was so nervous when I met the kids for the first time. Children are just so honest, no matter what. They won't let you forget if you make a wrong impression. And they *will* have an impression of you when you first meet them. You don't want them to say, "Poppy"—that's what they call my husband—"I don't like her."

When I met my future husband's kids, I learned from him that they were very nervous to meet *me*. He'd never introduced anyone he'd dated to them. He didn't think he'd marry the other girls and then they'd have to leave the kids' lives, so I was the first person they met.

My future husband had been divorced for five years when I met the children. We went to brunch at the Ritz-Carlton in Pasadena, and we played games at the table. The kids talked to me, which was so great. It was just so funny because I was so nervous, and instantly I thought, *These are such great kids! Oh my God, they're just little adults. And they're talking to me.*

They're six and ten now but were five and nine when I met them. I loved how even the six-year-old listened when I asked him to hold my hand because there were a lot of cars. I told him that we needed to do this for a reason and for his own good. He smiled and said, "Okay. Easy."

I think it's important to tell children why they need to do something, instead of just saying, "Get in the car now." Kids relate to a reason.

What I Know about . . .
Special Moments with Stepchildren

I did have a great moment on our wedding day. Tyler, the older child, took a bit more time adjusting to the idea that Daddy was getting married again than the little one, Carson. He had to deal with the fact that all of a sudden their father was going on trips and to lunch with someone, and they weren't going. My husband and his children are such good pals that they want to do everything with him. So the older child took more time to come out of his shell.

On our wedding day, Tyler was down on the beach in front of the hotel. He came upstairs to talk to me and called out, "Nonnie?" (That's what they call me—a combination of Nancy and Mommy.) He came from the beach and said, "I found something just for you. I think I was supposed to find this for you." Then he handed me this beautiful shell. He said, "I want to give it to you because I really love you a lot." The shell was in the shape of a perfect heart.

I took it and hugged him, telling him how much I loved him. Then I tucked the shell into my bouquet and put a ribbon around the flowers holding it. I showed it to him right before the ceremony. He looked like he was going to cry. That was a great, great bonding moment for us. (By the way, of course I still have the shell. It's on my desk, and I look at it every single day.)

I've been really lucky that Tyler and Carson are so well behaved. One of the reasons I fell more in love with my husband was watching him be a father. He treats them like little adults and not children. He explains everything to the kids. He isn't the type to say, "You should do this now." He'll say, "You need to do this because of *XYZ*." He really explains things to them. If one of the kids starts to sound upset, he'll say, "Use your words." That's the biggest key to anything when it comes to children: You talk to them. It's important that you acknowledge children's feelings.

What I Know about . . .
Telling Stepkids What to Do

Since our wedding, we've adjusted beautifully. I talk to the kids about having a stepmom and all the changes taking place in their lives. I'm starting to tell them what to do. In the beginning, it was best that my husband was in charge of the discipline and I'd back him up. It's very important to back up your spouse. In the beginning, as you're getting to know someone's children, it's nice to tell them who you are and what you'd like them to do, but in limited doses.

First, you make the bond with the kids, and then when they respect you, you can do more things. Yet I still let my husband handle the discipline, although now he supports me when I tell the kids what to do. It seems to work. I think it's easier that way when you back each other up.

Time-out

A quick story: I was in an airport once with my three young kids. I put a blanket out on the floor with all the toys on it. We had a long wait, and my wife, Rhea, went to buy magazines. I was on the blanket playing with the kids when a guy came up to me who looked like a bodyguard. He said, "Mr. DeVito, Mr. Red Buttons is here. He wants to say hello." I was a giant fan of Red Buttons, so I motioned him over. Red said, "Danny, I was watching you with your kids, and you look real good doing what you're doing with them. I want to tell you one thing: I went through therapy with my kids. We talked about all the time I was away doing movies or on the road for my comedy or in Vegas. In total, I took 15 years from my kids in days away from them."

I know that we have to work, be away, and do things that make life work. But you have to be aware that you shouldn't miss your children's childhood. Every single chance you get, you should be down on that blanket with your own kids. It goes by so fast.

*— **Danny DeVito**, father of Lucie, 23; Grace, 21; and Jacob, 19*

David Duchovny

Daddy Dossier

David Duchovny is a New York native who aspired to be a basketball star until an eye injury caused him to change his plans. He earned a degree from Princeton University before attending Yale to study English literature. He then switched gears and began his acting career doing off-Broadway productions.

David got his big break playing Special Agent Fox Mulder in *The X-Files* series, which reached cult-phenomenon status. On the big screen, he's had roles in *Kalifornia, Evolution, Zoolander, Return to Me, Trust the Man,* and *Things We Lost in the Fire.* He also wrote and directed *House of D.*

David and his lovely wife, actress Téa Leoni, are parents to Madelaine West, 7; and Kyd Miller, 4.

What I Know about . . . Taking Kids to School

I do like picking the kids up better than dropping them off in the morning. Leaving the house with kids in the morning? Man, they're slow! But what's fun about picking them up is when you see the kids before they see you. You observe them as people out in the world interacting as full human beings. I look at my daughter socializing and think, *She's a little person over there! And she's laughing about something! I wonder what they're laughing about.*

What I Know about . . .
Saying Naughty Words

We live in Malibu. There's this one area where you get coffee in the summer. There are a lot of paparazzi there. Téa gets very uptight because she doesn't like the photographers, while I don't care. They can take my picture. Whatever. But for her, it's really an invasion.

So the other day I was driving with my kids. My son was in the backseat, and he goes, "Daddy, do you know what those people are called who take your picture when you don't want them to?"

I asked, "What do you call them?"

He said, "A--holes!"

I replied, "Oh, really?" I didn't want to laugh in front of him, and I don't want him saying that word. Finally, I did respond, "We don't talk like that."

What I Know about . . . Surviving Kiddie Plays

Will my children act? Well, we go away to this place during the summers, and there's this kids' talent show. It's terrible because there's no coaching of the kids. I think that's actually great in a way because it's so natural.

My daughter wants to be in each and every sketch. She even did a gymnastics exhibition. It was cartwheels and somersaults for three whole minutes. Téa and I sat there and said, "That's our baby! Keep watching. It gets better and better!"

My son's sketch was holding up one of the letters of the town we were in and saying the letter. His job was to say "U." It was his turn, and he showed the U and said, "I'm not saying anything." I guess he doesn't want to be an actor.

*I was told I'd never have children, and against all
odds, I became pregnant. I had my daughter at 39
and my third child at 45. . . . By the way, my daughter
is an actress, but she doesn't want to work with me
for a while because she wants to be herself. But my kids
are particular about my work in one area—they just
don't want to see my breasts on-screen.*

— **Susan Sarandon,** mother of Eva, 21;
Jack, 17; and Miles, 12

Sarah Jessica Parker

Mommy Material

Sarah Jessica Parker is one of eight children who grew up singing and dancing. As a child, she studied at the School of American Ballet and the Professional Children's School. The little girl earned rave reviews on Broadway for her roles in *The Sound of Music* and *Annie.* She did her first TV special at the tender age of eight, and as a teenager she starred on the breakthrough TV series *Square Pegs.*

Sarah Jessica is best known for playing fashion icon and perennially challenged single New Yorker Carrie Bradshaw on *Sex and the City.* On the big screen, she has had roles in *Footloose, Mars Attacks!, L.A. Story, Miami Rhapsody, If Lucy Fell, The First Wives Club, Failure to Launch,* and *The Family Stone.* An astute businesswoman, she has a popular fragrance called Lovely, and Manolo Blahnik named a shoe after her, "the SJP."

Sarah Jessica is married to actor Matthew Broderick; and they have a son named James Wilke, 4.

What I Know about . . . Kids and Fashion

My son has some strong feelings, which I understand. Maybe this is unique to his age, but he's very concerned with what I should and shouldn't be wearing.

A few months ago, I showed my son the movie *Yellow Submarine.* I thought it would be better than certain other things he was watching. And that was it—he really connected with the Beatles. He knows every song of every CD and loves them. But he wants all of us to dress like the Beatles in *Yellow Submarine.* He'll say, "Mommy wear down pants," which means long pants. I do give him that one because it's so adorable.

Time-out

So this summer we were sitting around the kitchen, and my daughter was in trouble. Normally, it's my son—it's usually my son. But this time it was my daughter who was whining. David was talking to her, and my son sat there with this shit-eating grin on his face. He actually said, "Daddy, if I was whining, you'd be mad at me. But I'm not whining, so you should be happy with me." Meanwhile, I just sat there eating green beans and thinking one thing: <u>His delivery was impeccable. Oh, shit. We're in trouble. He's going to be an actor someday.</u>

— **Téa Leoni** on her expressive son, Kyd,
with actor and hubby David Duchovny

Felicity Huffman

Mommy Material

Felicity Huffman—nicknamed Flicka—was born in Bedford, New York; and grew up in Aspen, Colorado. She graduated high school in 1981 from the prestigious Interlochen Arts Academy in Michigan, where she majored in theater. She went on to receive her B.F.A. in drama from NYU.

Felicity was hired to perform with the Atlantic Theater Company, where she met her future husband, actor William H. Macy. Best known for playing the harried working mom Lynette Scavo on ABC's hit show *Desperate Housewives,* she has also appeared on the series *Sports Night* and *Frasier.* On the big screen, she has had roles in *Magnolia, The Spanish Prisoner, Raising Helen, Christmas with the Kranks,* and *Transamerica,* which earned her an Oscar nomination.

She and William have two daughters, Sofia Grace, 5; and Georgia Grace, 4.

What I Know about . . . Mommy Guilt

I think all working moms do an amazing juggling act. We do put a ton of pressure on ourselves. I know I feel like I'm failing every single day on every single front. It's tough to feel like you're constantly moving through guilt and failure and back again. In fact, it's crushing.

People ask me, "How do you feel about your character, a mother, going back to work on *Desperate Housewives?*" I think it's fantastic, because many women can relate to her balancing work with children. I know for myself I face that dilemma every single day. In fact, I just read a poll about parenting that asked what percentage of women feel guilty about mixing a job with motherhood—it was 87.6 percent who felt guilty. The poll asked what percentage of men feel guilty mixing a job with fatherhood, and it was near zero percent. That says it all to me.

Finally, a good friend of mine said words that broke the back of it for me. She said, "I don't feel guilty anymore. I work, and I spend time with my children. That's just my life; and although it can be tough, exhausting, maddening, and frustrating, I love it."

It's funny, but you're almost not allowed to say that it's really frustrating and even boring at times being a parent. God forbid, because you wouldn't be a good mother if you complained too much. You can complain about your husband, your job, and your friends, but you can never say a word about children and motherhood because if you do, then you have to quickly add a line about how fulfilling it is for you.

I think it's fine to get stressed out and say so, although I'm thrilled to be a parent. A friend of mine once said out loud that she hated giving her child a bath at night. But then she said, "But I love my child." She got stares for saying those words on the playground, but I think she should be given a break. Maybe she *doesn't* like giving baths!

What I Know about . . .
Competition among Parents

I try to be a great parent, but I've noticed a strange phenomenon: There's a competition among parents to be the best. I know there's this competition among mothers to breast-feed the longest. It's insane!

I was the youngest of eight kids, and I'm not even sure how my mother did it. Before I had kids, I thought my mom was tough. She had five kids within seven or eight years, and then the rest of us. It was crazy, but it was also a different time. Back in her day, you didn't have to be the perfect mother and breast-feed for the longest period in history. The litmus test was: "Are they alive at 18?"

Now you have to be perfect and well adjusted and breast-feed until they're 12. I like what Chris Rock says, "Are they alive and not working as pole dancers? . . . Then you've done a great job."

By the way, I do try to stay away from all of those magazines that give parenting tips, because it's just too much pressure.

What I Know about . . . TV Moms

Lynette on *Desperate Housewives* is happily married, and she's a perspective on motherhood that I haven't seen on TV before. We've watched the mothers on TV going, "Honey, you forgot your lunch money," "Doll, did you take out the trash?" We've never seen the crazy, maddening, impossible job of mothering.

I think Lynette makes real women feel great because her tough moments are acceptable and allowable. Before Lynette, TV mothers could only say that mothering was "tiring . . . but it's the hardest job I'll ever love." Of course, all of those things are true, but they pale in comparison to watching the true experiences of a mother. There should always be room on TV for real life, and women who are struggling to do it all and do it well.

When my son put his crayons in the microwave,
I learned how to buy new appliances. When
he flushed his crayons down the toilet,
I learned how to control my blood pressure.

— **Patricia Heaton,** the star of
Everybody Loves Raymond

Bill Paxton

Daddy Dossier

Bill Paxton, a native of Fort Worth, Texas, moved to Los Angeles when he was 18 to work in the motion-picture business. He began his career dressing sets for director Roger Corman and got his first acting job in the Corman movie *Crazy Mama.*

As a young actor, Bill had a role in *The Terminator* and then played very nervous Private Hudson in *Aliens* and vampire Severen in *Near Dark.* He's also known for his role as Chet in *Weird Science.* More recently, he has starred in movies including *One False Move, True Lies, Apollo 13, Twister, Titanic, A Simple Plan,* and *Spy Kids 3-D: Game Over.* In addition, he plays the much-married Bill Henrickson on the hit HBO series *Big Love.*

Bill is married to Louise Newbury and is the father of James and Lydia.

What I Know about . . . Nurturing

I believe the most important thing is having a relationship with your children when they're young, or you won't have one when they're older. I've seen friends caught up in careers. All of a sudden their children are grown, and these friends try to make a connection. By then it's too late in many cases.

Don't have children if you don't have time for them. They need a lot of nurturing and time—in fact, that's all they need. They need that more than toys or money or clothes. You can give them a cardboard box and they'll play with it if you're right there next to them . . . it's better than giving them some expensive toy and ignoring them. Just spend the hours, because it pays such a big dividend, and it gets better as you go along.

I've found parenting to be a very enriching experience. I'm glad to have a career, but I'm even more glad that I didn't miss the opportunity to be a dad. It's enriched my marriage as well. There's no bigger joy or reward for a couple than watching children develop their own intellect and find their self-confidence.

Believe me, my daughter has seen crazy things from me. But one day she came to the set of <u>Fun with Dick and Jane</u> and saw her father dressed up like a woman. She said, "Dad, no offense, and please don't get mad at me, but you're the ugliest woman I've ever seen in my life." Meanwhile, I'm standing there being crippled by stiletto heels and listening to my child critique her father. But then my daughter said words that shocked me. She said, "I have to leave right now, Dad, or this will do me serious damage."

— **Jim Carrey** on parenting his daughter, Jane

Cuba Gooding, Jr.

Daddy Dossier

Cuba Gooding, Jr., is the son of Cuba Gooding, Sr., who was the lead vocalist of the group the Main Ingredient in the 1970s (their hit song was "Everybody Plays the Fool"). The younger Cuba was discovered while break dancing, and even did a break-dance routine for the 1984 closing ceremonies of the Olympic Games in L.A.

Cuba's first major film role was in John Singleton's *Boyz N the Hood*. He received a Best Supporting Actor Oscar for playing football player Rod Tidwell in *Jerry Maguire,* where he coined the phrase "Show me the money." He has also starred in *Outbreak, What Dreams May Come, As Good as It Gets, Men of Honor,* and *Radio.*

He and his wife, Sara, have two sons, Spencer and Mason, and a daughter named Piper.

What I Know about . . .
Not Missing a Moment

I do love being a father, and I'm hands-on. I can't stress this enough to parents: They change quicker than you know. It will break your heart to realize that you went away for a weekend and your child said a new word or began to walk. As frustrating as it can be at 2 in the morning when they won't go to sleep, I remind myself that they'll be gone before I know it. All of a sudden they're crawling, then walking, and then running.

I hate that my boys are older now—9 and 11—and they're gone. I can't rock them to sleep. They won't lay their heads on my chest. My baby daughter is one year old, and I'm not letting her go. I want to cry because I've been gone a week or two, and now she's almost walking.

What I Know about . . . Men and Fatherhood

When it comes to parenting, women just get it. They're tuned in to it. For men, it's more about fear and providing for the kids. I try to tell my male friends to just calm down, sit on their fears for a moment, and enjoy their son or daughter. I tell them that there will be enough time to provide, but they can't live at the office. I tell them to spend an entire day with their children and to throw away the cell phone on that day.

Hold your baby for two hours while he sleeps, because you'll never forget that day. You might forget the deal that paid the bills, but when you're old, you'll always remember how your baby felt in your arms.

What I Know about . . .
Women after Childbirth

Let me break this down because I tell all of my buddies the same thing. Later on I hear, "You SOB, you were right."

Before the baby, you had this sex life with your wife. She was focused on you like diamond rocks were dropping out of your ears. But once she has that child, a big part of her time goes to the baby. This doesn't mean that your woman isn't still attracted to you, which is the first thing that goes through most men's minds. The truth is, her mind is focused on that little helpless creature in the other room. You're not the center of attention at this moment. You start feeling sorry for yourself and think that the love is gone. By thinking this, you're actually disrespecting your woman.

You have to remember that God has instructed her to take care of this little baby. She still loves you, but she's following nature by taking care of your son or daughter, which does take time—especially while she's getting the hang of taking care of this new child.

I promise you that it will switch back eventually, and the focus will swing back to you again. It's just that when women are given this gift of God's creation, they want to be the best mother in the entire world. Many women will even look back to those early days and say, "I was such a nut. I couldn't focus on anything but the baby." Just give your wife time to adjust and the entire family will benefit. Trust me on that one.

*I grew up with my kids in a lot of ways because
I was in my early 20s when I had my first child. What
did I learn? I think it's really about listening. I can remember what it was like to be their age—especially now that
they're teenagers. Put yourself mentally in their shoes for
a minute, and it will come back to you. Most of all, I try
to make sure that my children are heard. . . . But I don't
always listen. When my son said, "I want to drive,"
I just looked at him. Then I said, "What for? Take the
subway. Take the bus. You don't need to drive."*

— **Kyra Sedgwick,** actress, mother of two,
and wife of Kevin Bacon

Ray Romano

Daddy Dossier

Superfunny dad Ray Romano starred in and wrote the long-running hit TV series *Everybody Loves Raymond,* where he played pop and family man Ray Barone, the son of Marie and Frank Barone. Ray also voices the much-beloved woolly-mammoth character Manny in the hit films *Ice Age* and *Ice Age: The Meltdown.* In addition, he has had roles in films such as *Welcome to Mooseport* and *Eulogy.*

The Queens, New York, native is married to Anna Scarpulla, and they're the parents of four kids: Alexandra, 15; twins Matthew and Gregory, 13; and Joseph, 9.

What I Know about . . .
Rediscovering Your Kids

After *Everybody Loves Raymond* ended, yeah, I found out the kids were mine . . . just kidding. Honestly, I spent plenty of time with my kids during the show, but now I can do more things with them—go to more baseball games and more school events. It's really wonderful to be fortunate enough to take time off and spend it with your kids. I highly recommend it if you can do it.

What I Know about . . .
Being Your Child's Hero

I have twins who are 13, and also a 9-year-old. I'm their hero for sure, which is a nice thing to be in life. There's a good balance in our house because I also have a daughter who's 15, and she's into boys now, so we've lost her a bit in the hero department. But for the boys, yes, I'm their hero—and frankly, my wife has had enough of me, so it all evens out in the hero department. It is a bit of a battle to be Hero Dad in the morning because everyone hates getting up and getting dressed except my daughter, who's perfect and a straight-A student.

What I Know about . . . Mornings

I literally have to drag the kids out of the bed. I'm going, "Come on, come on! Get up!" I even give them piggyback rides to get out of bed—plus, I bribe them. I don't think this is great advice, but it does work. I've also found that when kids are having fun and know there's food on the table, then they'll get up.

What I Know about . . . Great Childhoods

I don't think kids care about houses or neighborhoods. As long as you have friends and you're having fun, then children feel like they've got it made. My kids have a ball, but so did I. I grew up without the big house. I lived in a neighborhood where you rode your bike and you went down the street and you had friends on the block whose mothers all knew your name. Most kids don't have that in this crazy world. They have big houses, playdates, and iPods. I think the simple way is the best way for children.

*When my daughter was two, she had a massive
meltdown at church, so I threw her over my shoulder
and headed home. Then some woman at the church
screamed, "That woman's stealing that baby!" And
as I walked the three blocks home, there was a small
group following me thinking I was stealing my daughter,
while others were walking by and recognized me
from television, saying "Hey, Soledad."*

— **Soledad O'Brien,** CNN newscaster

Shawn and Marlon Wayans

Daddy Dossiers

New York natives Shawn and Marlon Wayans grew up with their beloved parents, Howell and Elvira Wayans, and their many siblings—Dwayne, Keenen Ivory, Damon, Kim, Nadia, Elvira, Diedre, and Vonnie. The family is known for their hilarious work on TV's *In Living Color* and in several films.

Marlon has had roles in *Senseless, The 6th Man,* and *Requiem for a Dream;* and Shawn appeared in *I'm Gonna Git You Sucka.* In addition, the brothers were featured in *Scary Movie, White Chicks,* and *Little Man.* Both write and produce the hit hip-hop animated videos about good kids from the 'hood called *Thugaboos.*

Shawn is father to three children, and Marlon has two kids.

What We Know about . . . Raising Good Kids

Shawn: I have three kids—ages seven, four, and one and a half. I'm very hands-on. I'm not tough, but I do give the kids boundaries. I guess I'm still in the infant stages of being a parent.

I think the most important thing is that you have to communicate with your kids, but you also have to set rules and guidelines. In my house, you can't do whatever you want. I think as a parent you can't be friends with your kids too much until they get grown. You have to be their parent first, and you can shift gears later.

Marlon: I have a four-year-old and a six-year-old. I think the most important thing is to remember that they're individuals. You can't just teach them the ABC's. Every kid likes to learn differently. My son needed to learn his colors, so I took a bunch of plastic cars and I threw them on the floor. He doesn't love colors, but he loves cars. The key is finding out what they love to do, and then you'll always be happy.

What We Know about . . .
Getting in Trouble as a Kid (and What We Learned from Our Own Parents)

Shawn: We had ten kids in our house. My parents did this with no money. I was somewhere in between the troublemaker and the quiet kid.

As a kid, I took something from a store—it was a little *Star Wars* toy. My friends saw it, and they black-mailed me. If I didn't give them the toy, then they would tell my father on me. I didn't give it to them, and my friends did sit outside my house waiting for my father to come home. But my oldest sister was savvy. She told me to take the toy back to the store. I did that, and the lady from the store let me keep it. (By the way, my friends never told my father, but the fear of that stopped me from ever doing it again.)

Marlon: I stole a big bag of toys from a dollar store and stood outside and cried all day. I felt so guilty. It was freezing cold, and I had booger-cicles coming down my nose from all that guilt crying. But I never stole again because it was so emotional. I swear, if someone dropped $200,000 in front of me right now, I'd give it right back. I couldn't take the guilt or my parents being disappointed in me. Now that's good parenting when you don't have to say anything and your kids want to do the right thing.

I wanted to give my child the best gift my mother gave me, which is curiosity for life. I'm someone who's never been bored for a moment with life. Surviving cancer just illuminated those feelings. Life is too interesting. In fact, I've never had enough hours in the day: Oh my God, there's that book I want to read and that painting I want to draw. There's that person I want to speak to and that exhibition I want to see. There's a tree I want to go look at.

I learned that from my mother, and I need to thank her for that outlook. She was so interested in everything, and that's what kept her so interesting. She died at age 89, but she was still interested in people, things, nature, and life. My mother gave me that curiosity, and I hope I passed it on to my child.

> — **Olivia Newton-John,** music legend
> and mother of 20-year-old Chloe

Samuel L. Jackson

Daddy Dossier

Original cool guy Samuel L. Jackson grew up in Chattanooga, Tennessee. A graduate of Morehouse College in Atlanta, he established his career with roles in *Do the Right Thing, Mo' Better Blues,* and *Die Hard: With a Vengeance.* He played Jules Winnfield in *Pulp Fiction* to the tune of an Oscar nomination. His further credits include *Jackie Brown, Patriot Games,* and the *Star Wars*–prequel trilogy, in which he played Mace Windu. He also voiced Frozone in *The Incredibles* and starred in the recent film *Snakes on a Plane.*

Married to actress LaTanya Richardson, Samuel has a daughter named Zoe, 24, a graduate of Vassar College.

What I Know about . . . Backing Off

Parenting is one of those things where you learn to do it as you go along. There's not a book or map that teaches you how to do it.

I know one thing for sure: I didn't impose my will on my daughter. I only gave advice as advice was needed. I was sort of a hands-off dad in that way because I grew up in a very strict household. It caused me to rebel, so I gave my daughter the opportunity to make her own choices. I tried to just simply give her the right information. I think that works, because kids want to feel like they're in charge of their own lives and what they're doing. Of course there was discipline and consequences for doing the wrong thing. She had to explain what she was doing, but I didn't just stand there and say, "Because I said so." That's never an adequate explanation.

We were rehearsing one day, and we'd just moved into the theater and it was dark. I was onstage, and all of a sudden, I hear "Mama!" and Hazel had come in. In the dark just to hear this little voice—it's incredibly amazing.

— Julia Roberts

Catherine Zeta-Jones

Mommy Material

A native of Swansea, Wales, gorgeous Catherine Zeta-Jones got her start in musical theater and then became a huge star in her country for her work on the popular TV series *The Darling Buds of May.* American audiences—and Michael Douglas—fell in love with the dark-haired beauty after she starred as Elena Montero in the hit film *The Mask of Zorro.*

Catherine has also starred in *Entrapment, The Haunting, High Fidelity, Traffic, America's Sweethearts, Intolerable Cruelty, The Terminal, Ocean's Twelve,* and *The Legend of Zorro.* She won a Best Supporting Actress Oscar for playing vampy Velma Kelly in the film version of *Chicago.*

She and superstar Michael Douglas are parents to Dylan Michael, 6; and Carys Zeta, 4.

What I Know about . . . Being Overprotective

I'm constantly terrified about the kids. In fact, my husband, Michael, calls me Dame Doom! I'm always worried someone is going to trip and fall, or my son will fall off something and cut his chin, or my daughter will knock a tooth out. But I have to calm down, and so do moms like me, because kids will be kids. They're not made out of glass. They'll get cuts and bruises. That's a big thing for me—to just relax about it. I think you can make your kids crazy if you're too overprotective.

What I Know about . . .
Communication with a Laugh

When Dylan was going through his terrible twos, he'd have the occasional temper tantrum. Michael and I would look at each other and then look at Dylan. We'd say, "And the Oscar goes to . . . Dylan Douglas!" That always made our son laugh, and suddenly the tantrum ended. If you make a joke out of it and don't get caught up in the frenzy of a temper tantrum, then it will stop.

Time-out

I think the hardest thing about parenting will be letting go. It will take a tremendous amount of grace to let my children go someday. You know you have to do it, and I know I'll find it to be such a struggle. You just want the ability to watch over them all of the time, but that's not healthy. You have to let them make their own mistakes.

— Diane Keaton

Matthew O'Callaghan

Daddy Dossier

Animation director Matthew O'Callaghan has been making children happy for years. He directed the recent animated films *Curious George* and *Mickey's Twice Upon a Christmas.* He also worked on *Shrek, The Pagemaster,* and *The Little Mermaid.* He's the father of three children, ages 6, 9, and 12.

What I Know about . . . Curiosity

As a father, I realize that kids are naturally curious, and that should be encouraged. I'd watch my kids open a cabinet and take out the contents. They're not trying to make a mess, but they're just curious. Being curious is how children learn things. They'll disassemble a pop-up book to see how it works. They're not trying to break the book or be mischievous. They're interested in how things work, and that interest should be encouraged.

As a parent, you shouldn't get mad when kids explore. I've had cases where I go to put a DVD in and instead, a little doll has been jammed in there. When my daughter was young, she put quarters in my tape player in my car. Of course you get a little upset along the way. Parents should step back and realize that the kids are just exploring their world. So take a deep breath and say, "It's just a learning experience."

In hindsight, I think that it's easy to say, hard to do.

Time-out

People have asked me, "Should we take the kids around for Halloween? Should we take them to school?" My answer is always no, because as a mother there's always another way to solve problems. For instance, we were in India for Halloween. Brad, the kids, and I had an odd celebration in the hotel where we were staying. We had candy sent up and told the children it was from the saints. Brad and Mad were pirates. I put a big Afro on Z. I put on dreadlocks like Bob Marley. We just had the best time. As a mom, you just make it the best time.

— **Angelina Jolie,** a hands-on mom to Maddox, Zahara, and baby Shiloh (significant other Brad Pitt is also a hands-on pop)

Lloyd Allen

Daddy Dossier

Lloyd Allen is the author of the best-selling book *Being Martha: The Inside Story of Martha Stewart and Her Amazing Life.* He's the father of two children, Phoebe, 11; and Sam, 13.

What I Know about . . .
Fostering My Children's Talents

We live in a society where we want our kids to express themselves and realize their true potential without us as parents messing them up. How do you do this in the best way? I've learned that you have to stop and watch your children on an individual basis. Where does the child want to go with his or her own special talents? For instance, if my son doesn't want to be on the baseball field but I force him to join Little League, then I'm not doing him any favors. All you have is a kid who's on that field looking back at you and thinking, *Why me?* The same child might be in the garage trying to create a play—it's obvious this is a child who loves drama and not sports. It's your job as the parent not to force what *you* want on the kids, but what *they* want to do when it comes to their natural talents.

What I Know about . . . Teens

I'm dealing with a 13-year-old right now with full-blown hormones in motion. He hates me half, if not most, of the time. But I have to try to keep our connection and not lose sight that maybe my job is for him to hate me for a while. I didn't like my father for a while when I was a teenager, but that time passes. It's an endless battle that occurs with every generation.

It's not like you sit back during the teen years and do nothing. You still have to discipline your teenagers. My son can be willful, but he's very smart. One of his teachers even told me, "Don't worry about this kid. He's a huge-hearted human being."

Yet there are problems from time to time. I'll take things away—like the TV—for three days. My kids love the Internet, so that's a good one to take away for three days. I think the worst thing parents do is give a punishment like that one and then back down after just one day. I've learned that kids really do want those walls there. You know what it says? It says *love.*

It's hard to be the bad guy, but it gets easier after the first time. When your child says, "I hate you," it's quite painful. It's horrible and it hurts, but you should realize that it's not forever, and they don't *really* hate you. They're just mad at you and don't like to be denied the TV or the Internet.

One rule I have is that whoever starts a fight in the family must finish it. There has to be an apology at the end of a trying time. Someone must say "I'm sorry" at the end, and then you move on forever. Most of the time, like it or not, it's up to the parent to teach this type of mercy in a family. Even when the kids were younger, if I did something I thought wasn't right, then I'd tell them, "I'm sorry." I know I can lose it, and I definitely have my days.

My kids have learned this lesson, and they'll come to me and say, "I'm sorry, Dad." It goes up and back, in that I'll also apologize. If the *sorry* doesn't happen, then you chip away at your connection—and that's serious.

I would like to have a bath one day soon, and maybe pee.

— Sharon Stone

Blair Underwood

Daddy Dossier

Handsome actor Blair Underwood grew up all over the world in an Army family. He studied acting at Carnegie Mellon and then moved to New York City, where he immediately landed a role on *The Cosby Show.* At age 21, he made his film debut in *Krush Groove* and then did a stint on the soap opera *One Life to Live.*

Blair rose to fame in the role of Jonathan Rollins on the hit series *L.A. Law.* He also played Dr. Robert Leeds, a love interest for Miranda, on *Sex and the City.* In addition, he has had roles in the movies *Posse, Just Cause, Set It Off, Gattaca, Deep Impact,* and *Madea's Family Reunion.* He played Jackie Robinson in the film *Soul of the Game.*

Blair and his wife, Desiree DaCosta, have three children: Paris, 9; Brielle, 7; and Blake, 5.

What I Know about . . . Being Tough

I'm a tough dad. My dad was really cool, but there was discipline. We called him "The Man of Steel and Velvet." That's the key—you have to be tough but kind.

I try to pattern my fathering skills after him. In my house, my kids can't get away with stuff, but at the same time I love them like crazy and let them know that I love them. They also know that I have so much admiration and respect for children.

What I Know about . . . Sleep

Other than that, I'd say sleep now before your baby gets here if you're pregnant. A friend told my wife and me that when we were pregnant, and it was the best advice. When your baby is a newborn, you won't get much sleep at all.

What I Know about . . . Time Passing

One more thing . . . we're not in baby mode anymore, and it's nice to see time pass. We were in that baby mode for seven years, but now the high chair is gone and the cribs are gone. It's not sad, but rather a celebration that we're entering a new phase with the children. It's the next phase, where we don't do diapers in the middle of the night—and believe me, I did my share of diapers. Ladies, you should make your men be fair about that middle-of-the-night feeding and diapers. The guy shouldn't get a pass. It needs to be a team effort, and the children are so much better for it.

For five years I've been cooking a pot of stew.
The ingredients: love, patience, compassion, sacrifice,
respect, laughter, responsibility, obedience, God, and
sometimes even a few tears. He is yummy. He is
the love of my life and the purpose of my being.

— **Nia Long** on her five-year-old son, Massai

Dr. Wayne W. Dyer

Daddy Dossier

Wayne W. Dyer, Ph.D., affectionately called the "father of motivation" by his fans, is an internationally renowned author and speaker in the field of self-development. He is the author of 30 books; has created many audio programs and videos; and has appeared on thousands of television and radio shows, including *Today, The Tonight Show,* and *The Oprah Winfrey Show.* His books *Manifest Your Destiny, Wisdom of the Ages, There's a Spiritual Solution to Every Problem,* and *The New York Times* bestsellers *10 Secrets for Success and Inner Peace, The Power of Intention,* and *Inspiration* have all been featured as National Public Television specials. In addition, he has written two children's books, *Incredible You!* and *Unstoppable Me!*

Despite his childhood spent in orphanages and foster homes, Wayne has overcome many obstacles to make his dreams come true. Today he spends much of his time showing others how to do the same. He holds a doctorate in educational counseling from Wayne State University and was an associate professor at St. John's University in New York.

Wayne is the father of eight children: Tracy, Shane, Stephanie, Skye, Sommer, Serena, Sands, and Saje.

What I Know about . . . Young People

I try to teach my children that being successful isn't necessarily about performing a specific task, being in a certain occupation, or living in a particular location. It's about sharing yourself in a creative, loving way using the skills and interests that are inherently part of you. It can involve any activity: dancing, writing, healing, gardening, cooking, parenting, teaching, composing, singing, surfing—whatever. If the activities on the list are in service to others, you feel the bliss of purposeful living, while paradoxically attracting more of what you'd like to have in your life.

My daughter Skye is an example of what I'm presenting here. Skye has known since she could first speak that she wanted to sing. It was almost as if she showed up here in the world with a destiny to sing for others. Over the years, she's sung at my public appearances—first as a 4-year-old and then at every age up until now, at 21. She's also sung on my public-television specials, and the reaction to her singing has always been gratifying.

As a student immersed in a music program at a major university, Skye studied from academic and theoretical perspectives. One day in her junior year, we had a discussion that centered on her purpose and the silent inner knowing she's always had.

"Would you be upset," she inquired, "if I left college? I just don't feel like I can do what I know I have to do by sitting in a classroom and studying music theory any longer. I just want to write my own music and sing. It's the only thing I think about, but I don't want to disappoint you and Mom."

How could I, who tells his readers not to die with their music still in them, tell my 21-year-old daughter to stay in college because that's the "right" way, and it's what I did? I encouraged her to listen to the silent knowing that I've seen evidence of since she was a toddler, and to follow her heart. As Gandhi once said, "To give one's heart is to give all." This is where God exists in Skye . . . and in you.

I did ask Skye to make a supreme effort to live her purpose by serving those who'll listen to her music, rather than focusing her attention on being famous or making money. "Let the universe handle those details," I reminded her. "You write and sing because you have to express what's in that beautiful heart of yours." I then asked her to think from the end and act as if all that she wanted to create for herself was already here, waiting for her to connect to it.

Recently she voiced dismay at not having her own CD out in the world, and she was acting with thoughts of *not having a CD out in the world*—consequently, no CD and lots of frustration. I strongly encouraged her to start thinking from the end by seeing the studio being available, the musicians ready to collaborate with her, the CD as a finished product, and her intention as a reality. I gave her a deadline to have a CD completed that I could make available at my lectures. I told her that she could sing to these audiences, as she has done sporadically in her life, as well as on my public-television pledge shows.

Her thinking from the end materialized everything she needed, and the universal Spirit began to work with her unbending intent. She found the studio, the musicians she needed magically appeared, and a publisher agreed to produce the CD.

Skye worked tirelessly day after day singing her own favorites as well as several that I wanted her to sing at my appearances, including "Amazing Grace," "The Prayer of St. Francis," "It's in Every One of Us," and her own composition "Lavender Fields," which she sings from deep pride and passion. And lo and behold, today her CD *This Skye Has No Limits* is now out and is being offered to the public whenever she sings at my lectures.

As you can imagine, Skye's presence on the stage with me brings me so much joy and love!

Time-out

I said, "When you lie to me, I see a red Mommy dot on your forehead. Only mommies can see it." The other day I said, "Parker, did you push your sister?" He covered his forehead with his little hand and said, "No, Mommy."

— Rosie O'Donnell

Connie Chung
and Maury Povich

Parental Profiles

Connie Chung is the first Asian American and second woman to co-anchor the *CBS Evening News.* She grew up in suburban Washington, D.C., where her father was an intelligence officer; received her journalism degree from the University of Maryland; and began her career in the nation's capital. She joined CBS's Washington bureau, covering Presidential campaigns, Vietnam War protests, and several Presidencies. She has anchored for CNN and also hosted *West 57th Street.*

Maury Povich was born in Bethesda, Maryland, and is the son of legendary *Washington Post* sports columnist Shirley Povich, who worked for the paper for 75 years. Maury began his broadcasting career in 1966 as a reporter and sportscaster in Washington, D.C. He has anchored the news in Chicago, Los Angeles, San Francisco, and Philadelphia. He also anchored *A Current Affair,* the first syndicated news-magazine show, in New York City. In 1991, he became the host of his own talk show, *The Maury Povich Show.*

Connie and Maury have been married since 1984. They are the proud parents of a son, Matthew. Maury also has two grown daughters, Susan and Amy.

What We Know about . . . Everything Parental!

Maury: Okay, I believe I'm the disciplinarian in the family, but I know in the back of my mind that this isn't really true. Ultimately, Connie is the best in this department because she has such a loving way. It's funny, but the other day someone asked our son, "Who's harder on you: your mother or your father?" He said, "My father is easy." And I thought I was the tough guy!

Connie: Interesting, Maury. My thought is that it's all based on the first few years with your child. Those are truly the formative years. It's true, and I know this because I was there, which was wonderful!

Maury: You were there because you were fired from CBS! Honestly, a week later we had our child, and Connie stayed home for two years taking care of him. That was wonderful.

Connie: It was actually serendipity. I wish every parent had that opportunity to just stay home and be with the child. But I don't want to say that those are the only important years. I also believe it's very important to spend time with your child in the later years—like ages 8, 9, 10, 11. When they're toddlers, it's all about feeding, bathing, nurturing, and of course, love. When they're older, what they need is your input and guidance. Your job is far from over.

Maury: They're out in the world, and it's more important than ever to be close to your children.

Connie: When I worked at CNN, I was getting home at 10 P.M. I'd take our son to school in the morning, miss his day, and then Maury would put him to bed. CNN finally dumped me, and I was so glad, because it saved me from myself. I would have continued to work and work. But I've really been around my son from the ages of seven to ten, which has been so wonderful.

Maury: The bedtime struggles still go on. My wife puts him to bed, and they sit there and talk until both of them fall asleep. That's mental wet-nursing!

Connie: Maury! I plan on licking this before he goes to college! But if our son is reading this someday and he's at college, he can always call me on my cell phone.

Maury: Isn't there some child-rearing theory that you're supposed to walk away and let them cry? Frankly, I could never handle that one, although he never cried for me. He always wants Connie.

Connie: You couldn't hear him cry.

Maury: I don't scratch his little back.

Connie: Oh, that's wonderful. I love it.

Maury: Seriously, our son is the best thing that ever happened to us. Forget TV shows. Forget success. Forget the fact that we've made money. The greatest thing we've done together is to be parents.

Connie: We also have two daughters and grand-children. We have to mention them, too. We have a very full family, and it's a great situation.

Maury: How we found out about our son was amazing. . . .

Connie: It was really amazing when you think of the timing of it. We got our son when he was less than 24 hours old. He was ours, and this was very much meant to be. He was the right thing at the right time. I wouldn't have stopped work at the time. On Saturday it was reported in the paper that I wasn't working. On Sunday we got a call saying Matthew was our boy.

Maury: When we got him, he looked Asian to me.

Connie: He was just this beautiful little baby who was ours, and we both cried.

Maury: I'm an Eastern European Jew, and Connie is Asian. The kid is a breadbasket American.

Connie: We asked for a half-Jewish, half-Asian baby. They said, "Are you serious?" That was a joke. After we waited quite a while, this American boy came along. Matthew was destined to be our son. He was truly meant to be.

Final
Time-out

When you have a child, your relationship with
every child in the world changes. It's like you're in
a club you didn't know existed before a child came
into your life. I believe you should make the world
more beautiful for all children in any way that you can.

— Matt Damon

Afterword

Isn't it funny how so many people think that celebrities are so different from the rest of us? Surely they don't have to deal with the mundane problems and issues that we mere mortals do . . . do they?

Well, yes, now you know they do! Parenting is inspiring and meaningful and perplexing for *everyone!*

As you pored through the first-person accounts in this book, you no doubt came to realize that no matter what level of fame people have achieved, they're not immune to being challenged by the awesome responsibility of being a parent . . . just as you surely are!

So congratulations on being a mommy or daddy. Celebrity or not, you should be proud of yourself!

About ▪ ▪ ▪

Cindy Pearlman

Cindy Pearlman is a nationally syndicated writer for the New York Times Syndicate and the *Chicago Sun-Times.* Her work has appeared in *Entertainment Weekly, Premiere, People, Ladies' Home Journal, McCall's, Seventeen, Movieline,* and *Cinescape.* Over the past 15 years, she has interviewed Hollywood's biggest stars, who appear in her column, "The Big Picture." Cindy is the co-author of *Simple Things* and *Love Notes* (with Jim Brickman), *It's Not about the Horse* (with Wyatt Webb), *Born Knowing* (with John Holland), *Flex Ability* (with Flex Wheeler), and *I'm Still Hungry* and *To Serve with Love* (with Carnie Wilson), among other works.

About . . .

Jill Kramer

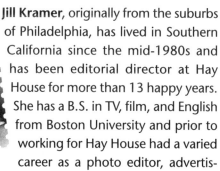

Jill Kramer, originally from the suburbs of Philadelphia, has lived in Southern California since the mid-1980s and has been editorial director at Hay House for more than 13 happy years. She has a B.S. in TV, film, and English from Boston University and prior to working for Hay House had a varied career as a photo editor, advertising copywriter, TV and film story analyst, newspaper columnist, and more. She's the author of *Catlove* and *Love Dat Cat* and writes social commentary for various publications.

We hope you enjoyed this Hay House book.
If you'd like to receive a free catalog featuring additional
Hay House books and products, or if you'd like information
about the Hay Foundation, please contact:

Hay House, Inc.
P.O. Box 5100
Carlsbad, CA 92018-5100

(760) 431-7695 or **(800) 654-5126**
(760) 431-6948 (fax) or **(800) 650-5115 (fax)**
www.hayhouse.com® • www.hayfoundation.org

❦

Published and distributed in Australia by: Hay House Australia Pty. Ltd.,
18/36 Ralph St., Alexandria NSW 2015 • *Phone:* 612-9669-4299
Fax: 612-9669-4144 • www.hayhouse.com.au

Published and distributed in the United Kingdom by: Hay House UK,
Ltd., 292B Kensal Rd., London W10 5BE • *Phone:* 44-20-8962-1230
Fax: 44-20-8962-1239 • www.hayhouse.co.uk

Published and distributed in the Republic of South Africa by:
Hay House SA (Pty), Ltd., P.O. Box 990, Witkoppen 2068
Phone/Fax: 27-11-706-6612 • orders@psdprom.co.za

Published in India by: Hay House Publishers India, Muskaan Complex,
Plot No. 3, B-2, Vasant Kunj, New Delhi 110 070 • *Phone:* 91-11-4176-1620
Fax: 91-11-4176-1630 • www.hayhouseindia.co.in

Distributed in Canada by: Raincoast, 9050 Shaughnessy St.,
Vancouver, B.C. V6P 6E5 • *Phone:* (604) 323-7100
Fax: (604) 323-2600 • www.raincoast.com

❦

Tune in to **HayHouseRadio.com®** for the best in inspirational
talk radio featuring top Hay House authors! And, sign up via the
Hay House USA Website to receive the Hay House online newsletter
and stay informed about what's going on with your favorite authors.
You'll receive bimonthly announcements about Discounts and Offers,
Special Events, Product Highlights, Free Excerpts, Giveaways, and more!
www.hayhouse.com®